Writing Power
ライティング・パワー

大井恭子
上村妙子
佐野キム・マリー

Third Edition
三訂版

Kenkyusha

はしがき

　従来の英作文教育では、英作文と言うと一文一文の「和文英訳」のことと考えられてきました。この「和文英訳」の弊害として2つのことが考えられます。1つは、「英語」と「日本語」というように全く異なる2言語の間に、一対一の対応があるように錯覚させてしまうことです。単語レベル、文のレベルであってもその対応には問題がありますし、ましてひとまとまりの文章ということになれば、発想の違い、文章の組み立て方が、2つの言語では大きく異なっています。もう1つの弊害としては、与えられた文を英語に置き換えてばかりいると、自らの考えを発表するという訓練ができず、「発信型」の教育にはなりません。

　そこで必要になってくるのは、「英語的発想」に基づく「英文ライティング」の指導です。この教科書は、したがって「ライティング」の教科書であると位置づけています。ライティングという作業は、「素材の発掘」、「アイディアの発見」、「アイディアの構成」、「文章化」、「推敲」という一連のプロセスを経るものです。さらに、大学生に知っておいて欲しい様々なジャンルにも注目し、ジャンルやパラグラフの展開法ごとのrhetoricや文法、語彙をそれぞれの章で学べるようにしました。

　また、この教科書のもう1つの特徴は「発見学習（heuristic learning）」を目指していることです。教材の提示はお仕着せではなく、学生に自ら「発見」させるように編集されています。そのチャプターのポイントとなる点を学生たちに発見させ、したがって興味を起こさせ、学習意欲が高まったところで教師による教授（teaching）となるように構成されています。また、練習問題も多く用意しましたので、それらをこなすことにより、学習内容の定着が図れるようになっています。

　英作文と言うと、その評価が難しいとよく言われます。課題として出された学生の作文の評価については、教授用資料に提示されているモデル作文を参考にしていただきたいと思います。また、教科書巻末のRevision Check Listを評価の基準として活用していただくことも可能です。

　なお、近年英語教育においては4技能を関連付ける統合的な言語活動が重視されてきています。そこで、今回の改訂では、各チャプターに示されているモデル文に音声録音を付けました。これにより、モデル文を「読み」、それを参考にして「書く」だけではなく、ディクテーションやディクトグロスなどの「聞く」活動や、プレゼンテーションやリテリングなどの「話す」活動と結びつけて利用することができるようにしました。

　この教科書は従来の英作文の教科書にはない新しい試みを盛り込んで制作しました。グローバル社会となった今日、英語ライティングでの発信能力の涵養は時代の要請であると言えましょう。ChatGPTなどAIを使ってのライティング教育も盛んになって来ています。そのような時代においても、自らがアイディアを発見するところからはじめるライティング教育の重要性は減ずることはないと信じております。

　出版にあたっては、研究社編集部の杉本義則氏、星野龍氏から貴重なご助言をいただきました。心からお礼を申し上げます。

2024年10月

著　者

本書の利用法

　本書の各 chapter は「ライティング・プロセス」を重視し、次のように構成されています。

　まず冒頭には、各 chapter で目標とされている学習内容を盛り込んだ **Model** を示しました。これにより、学生はいきなり「書く」という作業に入るのではなく、まず **Model** を「読む」ことによって学習内容をインプットとして吸収することができるようになっています。**Model** を読み上げた音声データがダウンロードでき、トラック番号がタイトルの脇に付してありますので、ご活用ください。

　次に各種の **Task** を用意しました。**Task** は本書の特徴の1つである学生自らによる「発見学習」を促す役割を担っています。**Task** は授業中に行い、学生に、後に続く授業内容にそれとなく興味を持たせ、「気づき」の段階にまで導くように工夫されています。

　さらに、「気づき」の段階を経た後に続くものとして、**Rhetoric** のセクションを用意しました。この **Rhetoric** の目的は、学生に気づかせたことをさらに意識的に学習させることであり、各 chapter で目標とされている文章を書くために必要な文法事項や文章構成の技法などが詳しく解説されています。

　次いで、**Rhetoric** で学んだ事項を「定着」させるための各種の **Exercise** を提示し、応用力を養うことができるようにしました。この部分は宿題として課すこともできます。

　最後の **On Your Own** は、**Model, Task, Rhetoric, Exercise** で学習した技法をフルに活用し、学生自らが「自力」で実際に文章を書けるようにするという、今までの教授内容を集大成する場です。課題は、学生にとってできるだけ身近なものとなるように工夫しました。

　さらに、文章を書くにあたっては「語彙力」の充実が欠かせません。そこで、各 chapter の最後に **Vocabulary** のセクションを設けました（ただし、10章と12章は除く）。ここでも章によって **Task** と **Exercise** を用意し、機械的な暗記方式による単語学習ではなく、学生が興味を持って主体的に学習できるような構成にしました。さらに vocabulary building 補強のため、巻末に **Appendix** として prefixes, stems, suffixes の表を載せてありますので、本章の中の **Vocabulary** の練習問題とあわせて利用していただきたいと思います。

　なお、教授用資料には、モデル作文が豊富に掲載されていますので、適宜ご利用いただければ幸いです。また、教科書巻末の **Revision Check List** を利用して、課題提出前の必須事項でありながら、とかく軽視されがちな推敲の作業を促していただきたいと思います。さらに、フリー・ライティングを行う際は、毎回巻末の**フリー・ライティング記録表及びグラフ**に語数を記録させ、さらなる向上を目指すよう励ましていただきたいと思います。

　この教科書を活用すれば、必ずや学生の「ライティング・パワー」は向上するものと自負しております。

Contents

はしがき iii
本書の利用法 iv
音声について vi

Chapter 1 Getting Started（英作文を身近に） 1
Chapter 2 Narration（時間の流れに沿って書く） 7
Chapter 3 Description (I)（場所を描写する） 14
Chapter 4 Description (II)（人を描写する） 20
Chapter 5 What Is a Paragraph?（パラグラフとは？） 28
Chapter 6 Essay（エッセイを書く） 35
Chapter 7 Process（順序よく書く） 44
Chapter 8 Definition（定義する） 51
Chapter 9 Classification（分類する） 58
Chapter 10 Comparison and Contrast（類似点と相違点を説明する） 63
Chapter 11 Cause and Effect（原因と結果を説明する） 71
Chapter 12 Argumentation（説得力のある文を書く） 78
Chapter 13 Letter Writing（手紙を書く） 86

［コラム］Story Grammar（物語を書く） 93
List of Prefixes, Stems, and Suffixes 95
Revision Check List 97
フリー・ライティング記録表 98
参考文献 99

音声について

　本書には本文中の音声番号に対応した音声データ（MP3）が付属しており、研究社ウェブサイト（https://www.kenkyusha.co.jp/）から以下の手順でダウンロードして聴くことができます。まず、研究社ウェブサイトのトップページより「音声・資料ダウンロード」にアクセスし、一覧の中から「ライティング・パワー」を選んでください。

(1) 上記から開いたページで「ダウンロード」のボタンをクリックすると、ユーザー名とパスワードの入力が求められますので、以下のように入力してください。

　　　ユーザー名: guest　　　パスワード: WP3OKS2024

(2) ユーザー名とパスワードが正しく入力されると、ファイルのダウンロードが始まります。PCでダウンロード完了後、解凍してご利用ください。

※スマートフォンやタブレット端末で直接ダウンロードされる場合は、解凍ツールと十分な容量が必要です。Android 端末でダウンロードした場合は、ご自身で解凍用アプリなどをご用意いただく必要があります。

※なお、ご使用の機器によっては、音声がうまく再生されない場合もございます。あらかじめご了承ください。

Chapter 1　Getting Started

自分の英語力を最大限に生かして、自分の考えをとにかく表現してみよう

1. フリー・ライティング

ライティングにおける第一歩は、何でもいいからとにかく書いてみることだ。フリー・ライティングは、英語で書くときの「イヤダナー」と思う心理的プレッシャーを取り除く良い方法である。

> フリー・ライティングのルール
> (1) 制限時間内に (5 分間、10 分間など)、止まることなく書き続ける。
> (2) 文法、スペリングの間違いなどを気にしない。
> (3) できるだけたくさん書く。
> (4) 消しゴムは使わず、ペンで書く。
> (5) 間違えたら線を引く。(例: I ~~go~~ went shopping.)

フリー・ライティングは回を重ねるほど効果がある。毎回語数を数え、巻末 (p. 98) の記録表・グラフに記録しておこう。前回より 1 語でも多く書けるように頑張りたい。

Sample 1

次の例文は、A 君が "What I Did Yesterday" というタイトルで 10 分間のフリー・ライティングに初挑戦した時のものである。

```
What I did yesterday

    Yesterday, I got up at the alarm was ringing at 6:30
and  I  got  up  at  6:45.  Then I washed  my  face
and   eat   breakfast.
    At  7:50,  I  left home.  I took  two  trains  to get
school.  And I studied there  to 4:00
                        about
    I leached at Hashimoto at 5:15.  It takes me about
15 minute to my house.  In my home,  I took  clothes
into  the  house , birds too, and cleaned  room.  At 6:30
                                                   From
I wached the TV program " CSI : Miami ".  It's was
interesting  and  I  look  forward  to watching it every week.
After My mother came home,  we ate dinner.  I went to
      bed at 12:15.                                 (104)
```

[1]

Task 1

Sample 1 にならって "What I Did Yesterday" というタイトルで、10 分間、フリー・ライティングしてみなさい。

2. プロセス・アプローチ (Process Approach)

ライティングというのは、1 回書いて終わり、ということでなく、次のような作業を繰り返してだんだんと良いものに仕上げていくものである。

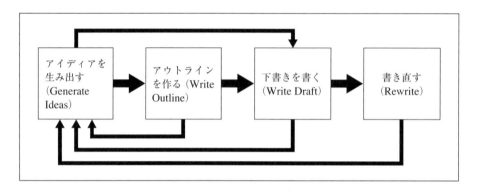

このようにして、いくつかのプロセスを行き来しながら、良いものに仕上げていくライティングの手法をプロセス・アプローチ (process approach) と呼び、この教科書の基本的な考え方である。

(1) アイディアを生み出す (Generate Ideas)

まず最初は書くべき内容のアイディアを発見することであろう。何を書いてよいのかわからないということは、書く内容 (アイディア) が乏しいことに起因する。ここでは、アイディアを豊かにするいくつかの方法を紹介しよう。

① ブレーン・ストーミングする (Brainstorm)

これは何人かの人でライティング課題のテーマに関して、自由に意見を言い合うというものである。お互いの意見に触発されて、一人で考えているよりもずっと豊かなアイディアが出てくる。

② 箇条書きにする (List Ideas)

テーマに関して、思いついたことを箇条書きにするものである。ただ頭の中でアイディアを練っているだけだと、せっかく思いついたアイディアも忘れてしまうかもしれない。文字にして紙に書きとめるだけであるが、せっかく思いついたアイディアはどのようなものでも書きとめておくことは後々有益になる。

③ グラフィック・オーガナイザーを利用する (Use Graphic Organizer)

アイディアを視覚的に検討するものとして、さまざまな形の graphic organizer を利用すると便利である。

ここでは「大学生になって、大学が家から遠く一人暮らしすることになった場合、アパートと学生寮とどちらに住む方をよいと考えますか？」というテーマで、さまざまな方法で自分のアイディアを広げていった過程を見てみよう。この時点では、英語を使っても日本語を使っても構わない。

1）表を使う（Use Chart）

	アパートに住む場合	寮に住む場合
よい点 (advantages)	・自分の居場所（individual space） ・共有する必要がない（don't have to share） ・自由に生活できる（live in a carefree way） ・規則がない（no rules）	・費用が安い（low costs） ・友達がいる（friends） ・安全（safe）
不都合な点 (disadvantages)	・家賃が高い（high rent）	・狭い（small） ・うるさい（noisy） ・往々にして古い建物（old buildings）

表にして書いてみると、アパートに住む方がよいと思われたA君は「アパートに住む方がよい」という考えに立ち、ライティングをすることにした。そしてもう少し、アイディアをふくらませたいと考え、クラスタリングをすることにした。

2）クラスタリングする（Clustering）

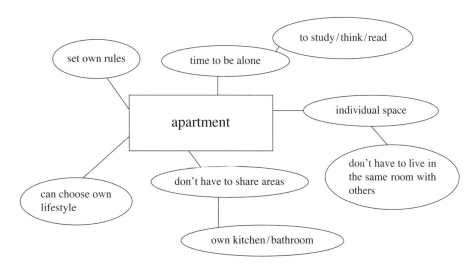

そして次に、クラスタリングで出てきたさまざまなアイディアをピラミッド・パターンとして次のように階層性を加味して図示してみた。このようにすると、アイディアの中で、何が上位概念で、そして、それを詳しく説明している下位概念は何か、ということがはっきりとわかってくるし、補足が必要な箇所も見えてくる。

3）ピラミッドパターン（Pyramid Pattern）

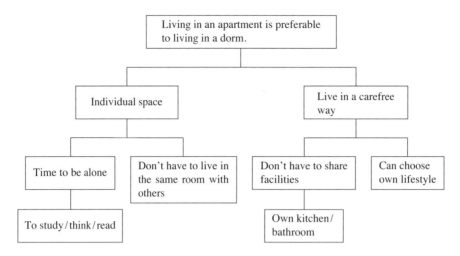

（2）アウトラインを書く（Write Outline）

ピラミッド・パターンまで来ると、アウトラインが容易に書けるようになる。アウトラインについてはこの後の課でも出てくるが、まずはA君のアウトラインを見てみよう。

I. Living in an apartment is preferable to living in a dorm.
II. Individual space
    A. No need to live in the same room with others
    B. Time to be alone
        to study / think / read
III. Live in a carefree way
    A. No need to share facilities —
        own kitchen and bathroom
    B. No set rules —
        make your own rules
IV. I would prefer living alone in an apartment.

ここまでくれば、あとは文章にするだけである。

（3）下書きをする（Write Draft）

Dorm Life or Apartment Life?

　　I would like to live in an apartment rather than a dormitory if I had to leave home to enter a college located far from my hometown. There are several reasons. First of all, having my own time is important for me. In a dormitory, sometimes two or more students have to share a room. I feel my room is the only place where I can spend time alone. It is fun to talk and spend time with friends, but I need time to be by myself. Second, I can live in a carefree way in an apartment. In a dormitory, some students have to share some facilities such as the bathroom and the kitchen. Thus, I may have to wait for a long time when someone else is using the kitchen. It would restrict my daily lifestyle. Furthermore, dormitories have many rules that would not allow me to use my time as I like. For these reasons, I prefer living alone in an apartment.

Exercise 1

「大学生になって、大学が家から遠く一人暮らしすることになった場合、アパートと学生寮とどちらに住む方をよいと考えますか?」というテーマのもと、A君とは反対の意見(「寮の方がよい」)で、
(1) 表を書いてみなさい (Make a chart)。
(2) クラスタリングをしてみなさい (Do clustering)。
(3) ピラミッド・パターンを作ってみなさい (Make a pyramid pattern.)。

On Your Own

(1) "What I did last weekend" というトピックで 10 分間のフリー・ライティングをしてみなさい。
(2) Exercise 1 で出したアイディアを、文章にまとめてみなさい。

Vocabulary — 英語の語彙の特色

Task 2

英語の語彙の中には同じことを指すのに、比較的やさしい言葉と難しい言葉の二通りの言い方がある。日本語のペアに対応するように次の単語の中から同じ意味を持っている単語を拾い出し、A欄にはやさしいほうの単語を、B欄には難しそうな単語を入れなさい。

> ask, build, inquire, give, think, purchase, construct, get, conceal, acquire, deep, present, profound, buy, consider, rise, hide, ascend

A欄	B欄	日本語
( ) — ( )	尋ねる — 尋問する
( ) — ( )	建てる — 建築する
( ) — ( )	買 う — 購入する
( ) — ( )	深 い — 深遠な
( ) — ( )	得 る — 獲得する
( ) — ( )	与える — 贈呈する
( ) — ( )	隠 す — 隠匿する
( ) — ( )	上がる — 上昇する
( ) — ( )	考える — 考慮する　　(朝尾、1985)

なぜこのように英語の語彙の中に同じことを指すのに、やさしい言葉と難しい言葉があるというように二重構造ができたのだろうか。その背景には英語の歴史がある。

11世紀の後半、それまでアングロ・サクソン民族（もとをただすとゲルマン民族）の言葉、英語が話されていたブリテン島にフランス語を話すノルマン人が押し寄せ、この島を制圧してしまった。征服者となったノルマン人達はブリテン島に住むようになったからといってアングロ・サクソンの言葉、すなわち英語を学ぼうとはせずに、自分達の言葉フランス語を話し続けた。したがって、支配階級の人々はフランス語を話し、一般の庶民は英語を話すという状況が生まれた。その結果、英語の中にフランス語の語彙がずいぶん入り、上記のような二重構造が英語の語彙の中に存在することになった。Task 2 では、A 欄に入る言葉が、もともと**アングロ・サクソン（ゲルマン系）**の言葉であり、B 欄の言葉はフランス語を含む**ラテン系**の言葉から英語に入った語彙である。

この英語の語彙に見られるゲルマン系 vs. ラテン系の対立は日本語語彙における「和語」と「漢語」との関係に似ている。私たちは、「手紙」と「書簡」、「形」と「形態」、「言葉」と「言語」などというように、和語と漢語を時と場合によって使い分けている。同じように、英語においてもゲルマン系の語彙とラテン系の語彙を使い分けなくてはならない。つまり、自分が書こうとしているものが手紙文（私信）のような口語文であれば、ゲルマン系の言葉を多用しても構わないであろうが、レポート・論文などの場合は、ゲルマン系の語ばかりを使って書くと、稚拙な文章になってしまう。アカデミックな文章を書くには客観性と高尚さを出すためにラテン系の語を多く使うのがよい。

自分の使おうとしている語がゲルマン系なのかラテン系なのかは、辞書を引いて語源欄を見るのがいちばん正確なやり方である。しかし数をこなしていくうちにある程度は察しがつくようになる。

Exercise 2

次の単語群の中から似た意味を持つ2つの単語のペアをつくり、英語本来（ゲルマン系）の言葉のものと、フランス語から入った言葉（ラテン系）とに分けなさい。

age, live, time, describe, child, soul, inner, despise,
infant, inhabit, interior, dislike, write, spirit

ゲルマン系の語　　ラテン系の語　　　ゲルマン系の語　　ラテン系の語
(　　　　　) ー (　　　　　)　　(　　　　　) ー (　　　　　)
(　　　　　) ー (　　　　　)　　(　　　　　) ー (　　　　　)
(　　　　　) ー (　　　　　)　　(　　　　　) ー (　　　　　)
(　　　　　) ー (　　　　　)

Chapter 2　Narration
人物の生い立ちを、順序立ててわかりやすく書く練習をしよう

　Narration は私たちにとって最も身近なもので、新聞記事もその一種である。Narration は chronological order つまり**時間の流れ**を軸としており、このため**時を表す語句**を使いこなす必要がある。

Task 1
次の例文はエジソンの生涯を記したものである。この例文をよく読み、時を示している表現に下線を引きなさい。最初の3つの表現にはすでに下線を引いてあります。

The Life of Thomas Alva Edison

　　Thomas Alva Edison is one of the outstanding geniuses in the history of technology. Edison was born in Milan, Ohio, U.S., on February 11, 1847. In 1854 his family moved to Port Huron, Michigan. There he began to go to school, but after three months the schoolmaster expelled him, labeling him as "developmentally delayed." His mother tutored him for the next three years, from 1854 to 1857, and aroused his interest in physical science books. In 1859, when he was twelve, he began to work as a newsboy on the railroad, and then he got a position as an expert night operator for Western Union Telegraph Company. After he gave up his position with Western Union, he started a business as a manufacturer in Newark, New Jersey, producing high-speed printing telegraphs. In 1876 Edison moved to the village of Menlo Park, New Jersey, to set up an "invention factory." At Menlo Park he created one of his most original inventions, that is, the phonograph, in 1877. Also at Menlo Park he invented the incandescent electric lamp in 1879. Three years later, in 1882, his Pearl Street plant in New York City was completed, being the first centralized electric-light power plant in the world. Edison continued to invent original devices. Among his 1,093 patents were included the carbon transmitter and the motion-picture projector. He died in West Orange, New Jersey, on October 18, 1931. Thomas Alva Edison is regarded as a folk hero who accomplished the American dream through hard work. He is highly respected because he embodies and perfectly fits his own definition of genius, which is a person who uses two percent inspiration and ninety-eight percent perspiration.

Exercise 1

下記の表を埋め、Edison の生涯を箇条書きにスケッチしなさい。

```
   WHEN              WHAT
   2/11/1847:        born in Milan, Ohio
   1854:             _____
   1854–1857:        _____
   1859:             _____
     │               _____
     │               _____
     ↓               _____
   1876:             _____
   1877:             _____
   1879:             _____
   1882:             _____
↓  10/18/1931:       _____
```

Exercise 2

あなた自身の生い立ちを振り返り、次の表を完成しなさい。

THE LIFE OF _____ (your name)

```
   WHEN              WHAT
   _____        ● born in _____ (where)
   _____        1. _____
   _____        2. _____
   _____        ● entered _____ Elementary School in _____ (where)
   _____        1. _____
   _____        2. _____
   _____        ● entered _____ Junior High School in _____ (where)
   _____        1. _____
   _____        2. _____
   _____        3. _____
   _____        ● entered _____ High School in _____ (where)
   _____        1. _____
   _____        2. _____
   _____        3. _____
   _____        ● entered _____ College / University in _____ (where)
   _____        1. _____
   _____        2. _____
   _____        3. _____
↓  NOW
```

Rhetoric — 時を表す表現

ここでは時を表す際によく用いられる表現のうち、紛らわしいものについて整理しよう。

Task 2

次の文のおかしいところを直しなさい。
1. I went to Hawaii in last summer.
2. My friend visited me in Sunday morning.
3. Can you repair my car until Tuesday?
4. My mother was in the hospital during four weeks.

(1) 日時を表す表現：at, on, in

at： 時刻などちょうどきっちりと表すことができるもの。

  6 o'clock   I get up at 6 o'clock.
  7：30   The store closes at 7：30.
  その他： at night, at midnight, at Christmas, at the end of 〜, at the moment

on： 曜日や日付など

  Sunday(s)   I will see you on Sunday. / We always meet on Sundays.
  July 23   I will leave on July 23.

in： 月、季節、年

  April   Schools start in April in Japan.
  1995   I graduated in 1995.
  (the) summer I swim in summer.
  その他： あとどのくらいかという時間を表すときに使う。
        Visit me again in three or four days.
        The bus will leave here in ten minutes.

 注意： (1) in the morning, in the afternoon, in the evening であるが、
       on Monday morning, on Wednesday afternoon, on Friday evening となる。
    (2) next, last, this, that がつくと、前置詞が省略される。
       We are meeting next Monday.
       I was in Europe last summer.
    (3) one, any, each, every, some, all がつくと、前置詞が省略される。
       You can come any day.

(2)「まで」を表す表現：until と by

until：ある状態がある時点まで連続していることを示す。そしてその状態がその点でおしまいになることを表している。

by：ある動作がその時までに完了していることを表す。

I was working until 8 o'clock.

```
                          5    6    7    8 o'clock
         ─────────── work ───────────────►
```

I want to finish this work by 8 o'clock.

```
                          5    6    7    8 o'clock
                                          ↑
                                        finish
```

(3)「期間」を表す表現： during, for, while

during： 「〜の間」というように名詞で表せるものの場合に使う。
for： 「期間」等、どのくらい長いのかということを表す場合に用いる。したがって、for の後には数詞がよく来る。
while： during と同じように「〜の間」という意味を持つが、during の後には名詞、及び名詞句が来るが、while の後には節が来るという違いがある。

There was an earthquake during the night.
It rained for three hours.
My mother was in hospital while I was away at camp.

Exercise 3

A. 次の（ ）の中に on, at, in のいずれか（何も必要ないときは×）を入れなさい。

1. I always feel tired (　　　) the evening.
2. I went to Spain (　　　) last summer.
3. I cannot come to your party (　　　) Sunday.
4. Will you be at home (　　　) this evening?
5. Are you busy (　　　) the moment?
6. Hurry up! The train leaves (　　　) ten minutes.
7. She calls me (　　　) every Sunday.
8. I will come to see you (　　　) the end of October.
9. My birthday is (　　　) July. This year it is (　　　) a Sunday.
10. I hope the package gets there (　　　) time for Christmas.

B. 次の文の（ ）の中に by, until, for, during, while のいずれかを入れなさい。

1. Can you repair my camera (　　　) Monday?
   No, I'll need to keep it (　　　) Wednesday.
2. Can you stay (　　　) this weekend?
   Yes, but I have to leave (　　　) Monday noon at the latest.
3. Although my mother told me to get home (　　　) 10 p.m., I stayed out (　　　) midnight.

4. Nancy did not get home (　　　　) 8 o'clock. (　　　　　　) that time, it was too late to go to the movie.
5. I don't like to stay up (　　　　　) midnight.
6. My mother stays home (　　　　　) the day.
7. We became friends (　　　　　) we were in high school.
8. We have known each other (　　　　　) seven years.
9. I usually study (　　　　) the week.
10. (　　　　　) the time I was away on vacation, my house was damaged by a typhoon.

Exercise 4

次の文は本文中の Thomas Edison に関する記述を書き換えたものである。(　)の中には、時を示す前置詞を入れ、下線部は、動詞を正しい時制に直しなさい。

　　Thomas Alva Edison (a) <u>be</u> still considered as one of the outstanding geniuses in the history of technology. Edison (b) <u>be</u> born (¹　) 1847. Instead of going to school, he (c) <u>be</u> tutored by his mother. He (d) <u>get</u> interested in physical science. (²　) twelve, he (e) <u>start</u> working as a newsboy on the railroad. (³　) 1876 Edison (f) <u>move</u> to Menlo Park and (g) <u>set</u> up an "invention factory". Hence he (h) <u>invent</u> the phonograph (⁴　) 1877 and the electric lamp (⁵　) 1879. (⁶　) 1882, Edison's Pearl Street Plant had been (i) <u>complete</u>. This (j) <u>be</u> the first electric-light power plant in the world. Edison (k) <u>keep</u> on inventing original devices. His patents (l) <u>amount</u> to 1,093, in which the carbon transmitter and the micro-picture projector (m) <u>be</u> included. Edison died (⁷　) October 18, 1931.

On Your Own

(1) 次の手順で、Edison の生涯を自分の言葉でまとめなさい。
　① モデル・パラグラフを見てはいけません。
　② Exercise 1 で完成した表を復習しなさい。
　③ Exercise 1 で完成させた表を参考に、自分の言葉で Thomas Alva Edison の生涯を英語でまとめなさい。本文をコピーしてはいけません。
(2) Exercise 2 で完成させた表を参考に、あなたの「自叙伝」を簡潔に英語で記しなさい。

Vocabulary — Vocabulary Building 1

Task 3

report という単語は 2 つの部分から成り立っている。どのように分けられるだろうか。

語源から学ぶ英単語

英作文を書くためには、なんといっても語彙の力が大切になってくる。これから 2 回にわたって語彙の力をつけるための、vocabulary building に取り組んでみよう。

今回は英単語の成り立ち（語源 = etymology）の知識を学ぶことで語彙力をつける方法を学ぶ。語源を中心にした「**語幹 = stem**」や「**接頭辞 = prefix**」「**接尾辞 = suffix**」の知識を蓄えると、意味のわからない単語に出会っても、ある程度意味を類推することができるし、語彙力を体系的に増やしていくことができる。

一般的にいって、prefix は単語の前について単語の意味を変える働きをし、suffix は単語の後ろについて、単語の品詞を変える働きをする。

Task 3 に出ていた report という単語を取り上げてみよう。report はラテン語起源の言葉で、re-（後ろへ）+ portare（運ぶ）からできている。この stem である portare が変化した port を含む単語はいろいろある。

例えば、re- の代わりに im-（= in）という prefix をつけると、import（運び入れる → 輸入する）になり、反対に ex-（= out）をつけて export（運び出す → 輸出する）、また、trans-（= across）をつけて transport（向こう側に運ぶ → 輸送する）となる。また、stem に suffix, -er をつけると porter（ポーター）となり、品詞は名詞に変わる。さらに、suffix, -able をつけて portable（運ぶことができる）とすると形容詞になる。

こうした prefix や stem の知識があると、未知の単語、例えば deport に出会ったとき、意味を推量することができる。deport は de- + port から成り立っている。de- は away とか down の意味を持つ prefix であるから、「遠くへ運び去る」、つまり「追放する」という意味であるらしいことがわかる。

このようにして、stem, prefix, suffix の知識があると、語彙力をどんどん伸ばしていくことができる。

prefix	stem	suffix	word
re- +	port		→ report
im- +	port		→ import
ex- +	port		→ export
trans- +	port		→ transport
de- +	port		→ deport
	port	+ -er	→ porter
	port	+ -able	→ portable

（他の例に関しては pp. 95–96 を参照のこと。）

Exercise 5　数を表す prefix

A. 1つの言語のみを使用する人を monolingual と呼ぶ。mono- は prefix で one、すなわち「1つの」という意味を表す。
次の意味を表す語を書き、各語の prefix に下線を引き、その意味を確認しなさい。

	語	prefix の意味
A1. 2言語話者	(　　　　　)	(　　　　　)
A2. 3言語話者	(　　　　　)	(　　　　　)
A3. 多言語話者	(　　　　　)	(　　　　　)

B. 上記 A1〜A3 の語の中の prefix を使った別の語をそれぞれ1つずつ挙げ、B1〜B3 に記入しなさい。
B1. (　　　　　)
B2. (　　　　　)
B3. (　　　　　)

Exercise 6　否定を表す prefix

not という否定の意味を表す prefix はいくつかある。prefix を加えて、次の語（形容詞）と反対の意味を表す語を作りなさい。また prefix に下線を引きなさい。

1. possible　　(　　　　　)
2. legal　　　 (　　　　　)
3. regular　　 (　　　　　)
4. important　(　　　　　)
5. smoking　　(　　　　　)

Chapter 3 Description (I)
場所を正確に、魅力的に描写する方法を練習しよう

Chapter 2 では時間の流れに沿って書くことを学んだ。この課では「空間の配列」(spacial order) について学ぶ。

Task 1
次のある部屋を描写している文章を読んで、下にこの部屋の様子 (家具の配置など) をスケッチしてみよう。

My Special Room

　　My room is small but very comfortable. To the right of the door, there is a dresser with a mirror on top. By the dresser, there is a nightstand. My bed is next to the nightstand, along the right wall. On the wall above the bed is a poster of my favorite band. There is a large window across from the door. The curtains have a bright
5　pink floral pattern, which match the bedspread and cushions on the bed. The round fluffy rug in the middle of the room is the same bright pink color. My desk is in front of the window. On the left of the desk, there is a media center. Along the wall opposite the bed, there is a tall bookshelf filled with books and my collection of wooden dolls. To the left of the bookshelf, there is an antique rack with many designer
10　scarves and hats. In short, I feel relaxed and refreshed when I come back to my special space.

My Room

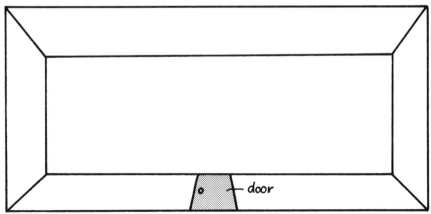

Task 2

上記の文で、何がどこにあるかを表している位置関係を示す語や表現に下線を引きなさい。

（例） by the dresser（ドレッサーのそばに）

Rhetoric 1 — 位置関係を示す表現

位置関係を正しく描写するためには、読み手がその場所を実際見ていなくても頭の中でその様子がわかるように、正確な位置を表す語句を用いなければならない。下記は Task 1 の例文に出ていない位置関係を表す表現の例である。それぞれの意味を確認しておこう。

in the front of	in back of	in the back of
close to	adjacent to	on the left

Rhetoric 2 — 修飾語

場所を描写する文においてはただ単に位置関係を正しく表すだけでなく、生き生きと魅力的に表現することも必要である。そのためには修飾語に工夫を凝らすことが求められる。名詞を修飾する場合、普通 3 つのやり方がある。例を a bookshelf で考えてみよう。ただ単に a bookshelf と言っても読み手にとっては正確にそのものを想像するのは難しい。そこで次のような修飾語を使うと生き生きしてくる。

① 前に形容詞（及び形容詞として機能する名詞）を置く：
   a <u>large</u> bookshelf, an <u>old</u> bookshelf, an <u>oak</u> bookshelf
② 形容詞と前置詞句で修飾する：
   an <u>old</u> bookshelf <u>with many scratches</u>
③ 形容詞節で修飾する：
   an oak bookshelf <u>which was given to me by my grandfather</u>

Task 3

次のそれぞれのものを描写する形容詞（及び形容詞として機能する名詞）を複数つけたいが、どのような順に並べたらよいであろうか。

1. a/an (old, oak, tall) tree → ＿＿＿＿＿＿＿＿＿＿＿＿ tree
2. a (white, cotton, new) shirt → ＿＿＿＿＿＿＿＿＿＿＿＿ shirt

あるものを描写する際、正確を期すために複数の語で修飾するということはよくあることである。その際、むやみやたらに並べていいわけではなく、ある一定の順序が英語にはある。次の図式は形容詞の並べ方の順を決める際に指針となる分類と順序を示している。

【複数の形容詞を並べる際の順序】

1	2	3	4	5	6	7	8	9	10
限定詞	→ 冠詞	→ 一般的形容詞	→ 大きさ	→ 形	→ 古さ/新しさ	→ 色	→ 由来	→ 材質	➡ 名詞

3の「一般的形容詞」と言うのは、pretty, delicious, intelligent というような『意見・価値判断』を示すものである。それに対して、4以下のものは言わば動かしがたい『事実』である。したがって、並べ方としては『意見』を『事実』の前に置くと覚えておこう。

（例）　most of the pretty little square new colorful American plastic toys
　　　　　1　　 2　　3　　　4　　　 5　　 6　　　　7　　　　　 8　　　　　9　　　10

　　　　a beautiful antique French doll
　　　　2　　3　　　　6　　　　8　　　　10

　　　　some dirty square white cushions
　　　　1　　 3　　　5　　　7　　　　10

Exercise 1

次の単語を正しい順序に並べ換えなさい。

1. wooden, beautiful, a, table, round →
2. ugly, orange, a(n), dress, polyester →
3. blond, long, beautiful, hair →
4. expensive, German, a(n), red, new, car →

Rhetoric 3 ― 存在を表す表現

Task 4

14ページの Model Paragraph の中から、「～がある」という存在を表している文を拾いあげなさい。

（例）　By the dresser, there is a nightstand.

位置関係を表す文では「～がある」という存在を表す場合、4通りの方法がある。
① 位置を表す副詞句＋動詞（句）＋主語
　　Next to the bookshelf is a dresser with a mirror on top of it.
② 主語＋動詞（句）＋位置を表す副詞句
　　My bed is to the right of the desk.
③ There is 主語＋副詞句
　　There is a small rug on the floor in the middle of the room.
④ 副詞句＋there is＋主語
　　By the window, there is a desk.

いつも同じパターンを繰り返すのではなく、さまざまな書き方をすると文が生き生きと

してくる。

> **Rhetoric 4 — Present participle and past participle**

　形容詞の他に描写力を高める効果のあるものとして、現在分詞 (present participle) と過去分詞 (past participle) がある。どちらも形容詞と同じようによく使われるものであるが、使い方に注意がいる。

> **Task 5**

次の文で（　）の中から正しい方を選びなさい。
(1) The movie was so (exciting / excited) that everyone was (exciting / excited).
(2) The lecture was so (boring / bored) that the audience was extremely (boring / bored).

　現在分詞 (present participle) の方は「〜させる」側であり、過去分詞 (past participle) の方は「〜される」側を表す。例えば、映画を例にとれば、The movie excited everyone. という関係がある場合、① The movie was *exciting* to everyone.　② Everyone was *excited* by the movie. と言える。どちらも日本語においては「おもしろい」という訳語が当てられるので紛らわしいが、どちらが「させる側」でどちらが「される側」かを考えるとわかりやすい。

> **Exercise 2**

次の文の（　）の中の動詞を現在分詞形か過去分詞形にしなさい。
1. Yesterday I had a very (interest) experience. I'm going to tell my mother about it. I'm sure she will be (interest).
2. After walking for an hour, I was very (tire). I don't want to join such a (tire) tour anymore.
3. Susan just found out that she got a D in her math class. She was very (depress). She became less and less (interest) in math. She hopes that she will have an (excite) teacher for the next semester.
4. Professor Rubin is always (annoy) by Tom's comments, but Tom has no idea that his comments are so (annoy) to the professor.

> **On Your Own**

あなたの部屋を描写しなさい。

Vocabulary ― 住まいに関する表現

英米の住居を説明する時に必要となる語句を学ぼう。

Task 6

次の絵は英米の家庭の居間と寝室を示したものです。各々の家具の名称を英語で表現しなさい。

A. living room

B. bedroom

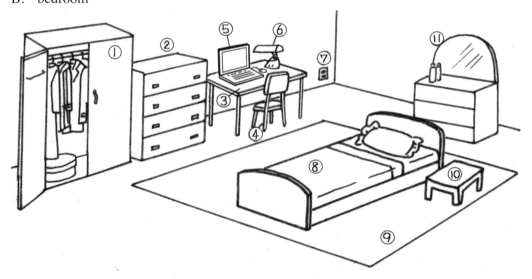

1. 英米の住宅

日本では住居の大きさは、「3LDK」とか「4LDK」といった具合に表されるが、英米では寝室の数をもとに、"3 bedrooms", "4 bedrooms" というように表される。英米の2階建ての家では、1階と2階の部屋の役割は異なる。1階部分は公の空間で、ここに住居の中心部分である居間すなわち living room がある。食堂（dining room）や台所（kitchen）も1階に置かれている。2階部分は家族の私的な空間であり、寝室すなわち bedroom が配置されている。物を収納する場所としては、屋根裏（attic）や地下（basement）が使われる。

2. 欧米の家具

最近欧米の家具が日本でも使われるようになってきたが、それでも、畳の上に座ることを中心として生活してきた日本人には区別の難しい欧米の家具もある。そうした家具の一例として「椅子」があげられる。

Exercise 3

次に示したさまざまな種類の「椅子」について、下記の各々の特徴をもっているか否かを検討し、例にならって違いを明らかにしなさい。（小島義郎、1988 に加筆）

特徴＼語	chair	sofa	armchair	rocking chair	bench	stool
① 1人用か。	＋					
② 肘掛けはあるか。	＋ －					
③ 足は固定しているか。	＋					
④ 背もたれはあるか。	＋					

Chapter 4　Description（II）
人物の外見や性格を生き生きと描写する方法を練習しよう

　人物を紹介したり描写したりする機会は多い。人物を描写する description では、読者が対象となる人物を頭の中でイメージしやすいように、多方面からその人物を観察し、多彩な表現を使いこなして、生き生きと、正確に描く必要がある。この chapter では、**人物の外見と性格を描写する方法**を学んでいこう。

Task 1

　進は、自分の家にアメリカ人留学生を招くホームステイ・プログラムに興味を持ち、アメリカの留学協会に問い合わせをしました。すると、協会から、Tom Miller という学生がやってくるという通知が来ました。以下の文章は、Tom の人物紹介を記したものです。Tom の外見、服装、性格についての特徴を例にならってあげなさい。

Profile of Tom Miller

　Tom Miller is an American college student. He goes to ABC University in the southern part of the United States. He is 18 years old. He is tall and slim. In fact, he is 6 feet 3 inches (190.5 centimeters) tall, but he weighs only 120 pounds (54.48 kilograms). His face is round, and his eyes are big and blue. He has dark, wavy,
5　shoulder-length hair, and a thick beard. He also has a dark complexion. Tom usually wears a T-shirt, jeans, and sneakers. In addition, he usually carries a backpack. He is a cheerful man and is easy to get along with. He likes cycling and going to the movies. In addition, he is interested in Japanese history, and he hopes to visit Japanese temples and museums when he visits Japan in the future. In sum, Tom is a friendly
10　student with many interests.

① Tom Miller の外見:
　18 years old,

② Tom Miller の服装:
　a T-shirt,

③ Tom Miller の性格、趣味:
　cheerful,

Chapter 4　Description (II)

1. 人物の外見描写

Task 2

バス停で4人の男性が列を作って、バスを待っています。1〜16の文はA, B, C, Dのうちのどの人物の特徴を示したものか、(　) の中に書きなさい。

1. He is of medium height. (　)
2. He has a dark complexion. (　)
3. His hair is long. (　)
4. He has a beard and moustache. (　)
5. He is heavy-set. (　)
6. He is in his sixties. (　)
7. He has a scar on his right arm. (　)
8. He is wearing a striped jacket. (　)
9. His face is round. (　)
10. He has a tie on. (　)
11. He is slim. (　)
12. He has an umbrella in his right hand. (　)
13. He is wearing a sweat suit. (　)
14. His eyes are big. (　)
15. He is wearing a polka-dotted shirt. (　)
16. He is bald. (　)

Rhetoric 1 ── 人物の外面的描写に関わる表現

次の表は人物の外面的描写に必要な項目をまとめたものである。各々の語(句)の意味を確認しなさい。

age　　young, middle-aged, elderly, old
　　　　　in one's teens, 20s, 30s, 40s

	in one's early/mid/late teens, 20s, 30s, 40s
height	tall, short, (of) medium/average height
build	fat, heavy-set, stout, plump, well-built
	thin, slim, slender, skinny
	(of) medium/average build
face	thin, long, square, round, triangular
nose	flat, broad, prominent, turned-up
eyes	big, small, round, narrow, almond-shaped
	blue, brown, gray, hazel, dark
hair	long, short, shoulder-length, chin-length
	straight, curly, frizzy, wavy, permed
	thick, thin, bald, parted on the side
	black, brown, dark, blond, gray, white, salt and pepper
others	wrinkles, single/double eyelids, scar, mole, beard, moustache, whiskers,
	rosy cheeks, high cheekbones, pointed jaw, freckles
	dark/light complexion
clothes	T-shirt, shirt, sweatshirt, blouse, sweater, jacket, coat
	jeans, pants, trousers, skirt
	suit, sweat suit, dress
	tie, scarf, cap, hat, earrings, pendant, glasses, bracelet, necklace
	high-heels, sneakers, boots, sandals
patterns	polka-dotted, checked, plaid, striped, flower-patterned, paisley print

Rhetoric 2 ── 人物の外面的描写に関わる表現

　人物の外観を描写するには、いくつかの基本的な文型がある。いつも同じパターンを使うと読者は退屈してしまうので変化をつける必要がある。
(1) 身体の特徴について
　① BE 動詞を使った表現：　体の部分＋BE 動詞＋形容詞
　　　　　　　　　　　　　　Her hair　　*is*　　long and curly.
　② HAVE を使った表現：　主語＋HAVE 動詞＋(冠詞)＋形容詞＋体の部分
　　　　　　　　　　　　　　She　　*has*　　　　long, curly hair.
　　　　　　　　　　　　　　She　　*has*　　a　short, turned-up nose.
(2) 身につけているものについて
　① WEAR を使った表現：　　She *wears* jeans.
　② HAVE ON を使った表現：　She *has* jeans *on*.

Rhetoric 3 — 紛らわしい表現

(1) WEAR にはさまざまな意味がある。
　　スーツを着ている。　　　　*wear* a suit
　　スカートをはいている。　　*wear* a skirt
　　帽子をかぶっている。　　　*wear* a hat
　　スカーフをつけている。　　*wear* a scarf
　　眼鏡をかけている。　　　　*wear* glasses

(2) 状態を表す動詞と動作を表す動詞
　　wear, have on：「身につけている」状態を表す
　　put on（動作）：「着る」という動作を表す
　　● Tom usually *wears* / *has on* a T-shirt and jeans, but he *is wearing* a suit today because he is going to a party.
　　● I *put on* a jacket before I went out because it was rather cold outside.

Exercise 1

次の空所に、wear, have on, put on のいずれかを適切な形にして入れなさい。
(1) It is not easy for most Japanese girls to (　　　) a kimono by themselves.
(2) She doesn't usually (　　　) much makeup.
(3) My brother usually (　　　) glasses, but now he is (　　　) contact lenses because he is going to attend a wedding reception.
(4) She (　　　) lipstick before she went to work.
(5) Please (　　　) your jacket. It's quite cold in here.

Exercise 2

次の注意事項に気をつけて Mr. David Brown を描写しなさい。
① Model Paragraph (p. 20) を参考にし、箇条書きに文を並べるのではなく、paragraph の形にまとめること。
② Rhetoric 1 で学んだ人物描写に関わる表現と Rhetoric 2, 3 で学んださまざまな文型を活用すること。
③ 形容詞の並べ方は、Chapter 3 の Rhetoric 2 (p. 16) を参照すること。

2. 人物の性格描写

人物の描写には、外見だけではなく性格も関わってくる。そこで性格を表す形容詞などの表現を学ぶ必要がある。

Task 3

下に示した表現は、血液型にまつわる性格的な特徴を示したものである。それぞれの表現の意味を考えながら、長所を表していると思われるものには＋を、短所を表していると思われるものには－を（　）の中に記入しなさい。

Type A：
( )　diligent
( )　dependent
( )　nervous
( )　responsible
( )　have a strong sense of justice
( )　inflexible

Type O：
( )　boastful
( )　energetic
( )　bossy
( )　open-minded
( )　possessive
( )　have good concentration

Type B：
( )　creative
( )　restless
( )　moody
( )　positive
( )　inconsiderate
( )　sociable

Type AB：
( )　intelligent
( )　peace-loving
( )　act tactfully
( )　capricious
( )　have strong likes and dislikes
( )　sincere

Exercise 3

Task 3 の解答をもとに、下記の下線部を埋め、paragraph を完成しなさい。

　　It is said that people have different personalities depending on their blood types. My blood type is ¹___. We have some good points. We are thought to ²_____. On the other hand, we have certain bad points. For instance, we are considered to ³_____. I think I can get along with Type ⁴___ people because they are said to ⁵_____. However, I do not think I can get along with Type ⁶___ people, who are supposed to ⁷_____.

Rhetoric 4 ― 人物の性格描写に関わる表現

　性格についての表現は、その表現と類似した意味を持つ表現や、反対の意味を持つ表現を一緒に調べ、学ぶと豊かになる。例えば、"kind" という表現を学ぶ際には、その類義語である "gentle" や "warm-hearted"、また反対語の "cold" や "inconsiderate" などを一緒に学ぶとよいだろう。ただし、類義語には微妙な意味の差があるので注意がいる。

Exercise 4

次の語の反対語を下記の語群より選びなさい。

1) shy： _____   6) selfish： _____
2) cruel： _____   7) easy-going： _____
3) impatient： _____ 8) trustworthy： _____
4) gloomy： _____   9) extroverted： _____
5) optimistic： _____ 10) lazy： _____

hardworking	cheerful	kind	unreliable
tolerant	pessimistic	jealous	uptight
introverted	considerate	outgoing	arrogant

On Your Own

あなたはアメリカ人のBrownさんの家庭にホームステイをすることになりました。Brown家の人々はあなたを空港まで迎えにきてくれると言っています。あなたとBrown家の人々はこれまでに会ったことがないので、あなたは自己紹介のEメールを書くことになりました。この課で学んだ表現や文型を活用して、あなたの外見、性格を記した自己紹介のメールを書きなさい。

Dear Mr. & Mrs. Brown and Family,

Thank you very much for allowing me to stay at your home during the coming vacation.
Since we have never met, I would like to introduce myself.

I am a _____ at _____ College / University in _____ in Japan.

　　［ あなたの外見について ］

Please find an attached photo of me.

　　［ あなたの性格、趣味について ］

My email address is: _____
I am looking forward to meeting all of you.

Sincerely yours,

_____

Vocabulary — Synonyms

この chapter では人物を表すさまざまな形容詞を学んだ。それらの中には表す意味が似通ったいくつかの形容詞もあった。同じような意味を持つ語のことを「類義語」(synonyms) という。

Task 4

次に示したのは「太っている」という意味を表す類義語と「やせている」という意味を表す類義語である。それぞれどういう違いがあるのだろうか。自分が言われたとき、いやな気分がするのはどれだろうか。また、他人に対し、失礼にならない語はどれだろうか。

「太っている」	「やせている」
fat	thin
obese	lean
chubby	slim
plump	slender
stout	skinny

Denotation と Connotation

以上見てきたように、同じ意味を持つ類義語でもその意味合いはさまざまであることがわかる。このような差を表すのに、**辞書的な意味を denotation** といい、それぞれの単語のかもし出す微妙な意味合いを **connotation** という。

また、あまりにも直接的な語は、オブラートに包んで別の表現を使う。例えば、die (死ぬ) という直接的な響きを避けて、pass away (亡くなる) を使ったり、toilet の代わりに、アメリカ英語では bathroom (欧米では風呂場にトイレもあるので) を使ったりする。このような遠回しの言い方を婉曲語法 (euphemism) といい、近年アメリカでは "PC" (politically correct) との関連で差別や偏見にもとづかない「政治的に正しい」さまざまな言い方が生み出されている。

Exercise 5

次の A 群〜E 群の各語は denotation は同一であるが、connotation がそれぞれ、好ましくない (unfavorable)、中立 (neutral)、好意的 (favorable) というように異なっているものである。それぞれの語群の中で、connotaion を考えて (あるいは辞書を調べて) 順に並べてみよう。また、その意味合いの違いはどこからくるものかについても考えてみよう。さらに、日本語の意味ではどのようになるかも考えよう。

	unfavorable	neutral	favorable
(A)	_____	_____	_____
(B)	_____	_____	_____
(C)	_____	_____	_____
(D)	_____	_____	_____
(E)	_____	_____	_____

（A群）police officer, guardian of the law, cop
（B群）mercy killing, legal murder, euthanasia
（C群）burden, opportunity for achievement, task
（D群）crazy, psychotic, mentally unbalanced
（E群）cancer, lingering illness, carcinoma

Exercise 6

次にあげる語を婉曲表現で表すとするとどれが適当か、下から選んで（ ）の中に書き入れなさい。また、なぜそういった言い換えが必要なのか、考えてみよう。（朝尾、1985 より）

1. old people　　（　　　）
2. salesman　　（　　　）
3. alcoholic　　（　　　）
4. poor people　（　　　）
5. cheap　　　　（　　　）
6. unemployed　（　　　）
7. garbage collector　（　　　）
8. stewardess　（　　　）
9. races　　　　（　　　）
10. bankruptcy　（　　　）
11. breast　　　（　　　）
12. janitor　　　（　　　）

---

inexpensive, custodial engineer, problem drinker, between jobs, sanitary engineer, sales representative, senior citizens, ethnic groups, cabin attendant, chest, underprivileged people, financial straits

Chapter 5　What Is a Paragraph?
Paragraph について理解しよう

これまでにも 1 つのまとまりを持った文章、つまり paragraph を見てきたが、ここでは詳しく paragraph の構成、及び良い paragraph を書くためのポイントを学んでいく。

Task 1

次の文章はファミリー・レストランの利点について述べているものである。いくつの利点が述べられているか、またどのような利点が述べられているかを確認しなさい。

Family Restaurants

　　Family restaurants are popular among families for several reasons. First of all, their opening hours and locations are convenient. Many of them are open till late at night and all year round; therefore, we can go there whenever we want. Moreover, many family restaurants are located in easily accessible places such as near a train station or on a highway, so we can go there either on foot or by car easily. Second, family restaurants are typically more spacious than other types of restaurants. This helps to reduce the waiting time or probability of not being able to get a reservation for your choice of date or time. Finally, their popularity among families lies in the variety on the menus. Many types of dishes and set courses can be ordered from a wide selection besides Japanese food, such as Chinese, Italian or American. I like home cooking rather than restaurant food. Furthermore, the wide assortment of dishes on the menu also allows for choice in how much the family wants to spend on their meal. In conclusion, families often choose family-style restaurants when dining out because they are convenient, spacious, and attractive in the variety of dishes they offer.

●家族にとってのファミリー・レストランの利点

_____

_____

_____

Chapter 5　What Is a Paragraph?　29

1.　Paragraph（パラグラフ）とは...

(1) 英語の文章の基本的な単位である。
(2) 冒頭の文は 3〜5 文字スペースを空けてから書き始める。これを indention という（図 1 参照）。
(3) 1 文ごとに改行せず、複数の文からなる文章の形式である（図 1 参照）。
(4) 次の 3 つの部分から成る（図 2 参照）。
　① **Topic Sentence**（トピック・センテンス）
　② **Supporting Sentences**（支持文）
　③ **Concluding Sentence(s)**（結論文）

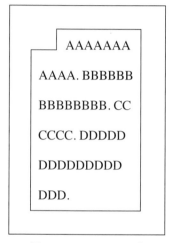
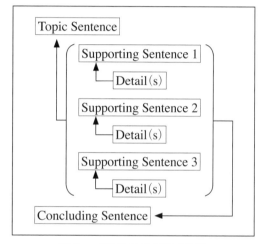

図 1　パラグラフの形　　図 2　パラグラフの基本構造

2.　Topic Sentence とは...

(1) Paragraph 全体の論旨を述べた文である。
(2) 通常 **paragraph** の冒頭に置かれることが多い。
(3) Paragraph が「何について」書かれているかを示した **topic**（主題）と、その主題に対して「筆者がどのような意見」を持っているのかという **controlling idea** から成り立っている。
(4) 次のような文は topic sentence としては不適切である。
　① Topic だけで controlling idea がないもの
　　（例えば、I am going to talk about family restaurants.）
　② Paragraph の topic sentence としては内容が大きすぎるもの
　　（例えば、Japan is different from other countries in many respects.）
　③ 単に事実を述べただけで筆者の意見を記していないもの
　　（例えば、Family restaurants are restaurants mainly for families.）

Exercise 1

次のそれぞれの文が topic sentence として適切であるかを判断しなさい。

1) 適切と思われる文については、topic をマルで囲み、controlling idea には下線を引きなさい。
2) 不適切と思われる文については、なぜ不適切なのかの理由を考えなさい。

1. English is a language spoken in the U.S.A. and the UK.
2. I am going to write about English.
3. Studying English at university is important for Japanese students for several reasons.
4. Modern Japan faces a lot of problems.

Exercise 2

1) Model Paragraph (p. 28) の topic sentence を探し出しなさい。
2) Topic sentence はどこに置かれていますか。
3) Topic をマルで囲みを、controlling idea には下線を引きなさい。

Exercise 3

1) Chapter 2 と Chapter 3 の Model Paragraph (p. 7, 14) において、それぞれの topic sentence を探し出しなさい。
2) topic sentence がそれぞれの Model Paragraph のどこに置かれていますか。
3) また、それぞれの topic sentence について、topic をマルで囲みを、controlling idea には下線を引きなさい。

Exercise 4

次の topic で paragraph を書くとした場合、このままでは良い topic sentence とは言えない。より良い topic sentence に書き換えなさい。

1. Camping is fun.（ヒント：誰にとって？）

2. It is difficult to become good at English.（ヒント：英語のどの部分が？）

3. Supporting Sentences とは...

(1) Topic sentence に示された筆者の主張の正当性を具体的に説明する文を指す。
(2) したがって、topic sentence が総括的 (**general**) であるのに対し、supporting sentences はより具体的 (**concrete**) かつ個別的 (**specific**) である。
(3) Supporting Sentence 1, Supporting Sentence 2, Supporting Sentence 3 というように複数の文から成る。
(4) 各 supporting sentence は、さらに **detail(s)** によって具体的に説明されている。

(5) したがって、topic sentence は supporting sentences によって支えられ、supporting sentence は detail(s) によって支えられるという**有機的な構造**になっている（図2参照）。
(6) Supporting sentences は **First, Second, Finally** のようなつなぎ言葉によって導入されることが多い。

Exercise 5
Model Paragraph の supporting sentences を拾い出し、二重線を引きなさい。また、おのおのの supporting sentence を具体的に説明している detail(s) に波線を引きなさい。

Exercise 6
Model Paragraph においてそれぞれの supporting sentence を導入しているつなぎ言葉をマルで囲みなさい。

4. Concluding Sentence とは...

(1) Paragraph の終わりに置かれる。
(2) Paragraph 全体を**総括して要約し、締めくくる**。
(3) Topic sentence で述べられた筆者の考えを**別の言葉で言い換える**。
(4) Concluding sentence は **In conclusion, In summary** などの語句で始められることが多い。

Exercise 7
1) Model Paragraph における concluding sentence を探しなさい。
2) Concluding sentence は paragraph のどこに置かれていますか。
3) また、どのようなつなぎ言葉によって導入されていますか。

Exercise 8
次の文章は paragraph についてまとめたものである。これまでに学んだことから考えて空所1〜9に適語を選んで入れなさい。

  A paragraph has (¹) major parts. The (²) part is the (³). It consists of a (⁴) and a (⁵). The topic sentence is developed by (⁶), which are further supported by (⁷). The (⁸) summarizes the paragraph. These are the major (⁹) of a paragraph.

> supporting sentences, controlling idea, topic sentence
> first, details, three, concluding sentence, topic, parts

Exercise 9

Paragraph について学んだことをもとに、下記に示した表の空所を埋め、Model Paragraph の構造を示しなさい。

Topic Sentence	Family restaurants are popular among families for several reasons.		
Supporting Sentences	**Supporting Sentence 1**	Their opening hours and locations are (¹).	
	Detail 1	Open (²) (³) at night and all year round	
	Detail 2	Located in easily (⁴) places	
	Supporting Sentence 2	They are typically more (⁵) than other types of restaurants.	
	Detail 1	Less (⁶) time	
	Detail 2	Less (⁷) of not being able to get a (⁸)	
	Supporting Sentence 3	They are characterized by the variety on the menus.	
	Detail 1	Choice in what to (⁹) from a wide selection	
	Detail 2	Choice in how much to (¹⁰) on the meal	
Concluding Sentence	Families often choose family-style restaurants when dining out because they are convenient, spacious, and attractive in the variety of dishes they offer.		

5. 良い paragraph を書くためには...

良い paragraph を書くには、paragraph 構成に必要な3つの要素（topic sentence, supporting sentences, concluding sentence）をしっかりと書くほかに、以下の点に注意する必要がある。

(1) 統一性 (unity)

Paragraph という単位における意味のまとまりは特に「統一性」と呼ばれている。すなわち、**1つの paragraph の中では1つの主張に関することだけが述べられていなければならない**。もし、topic sentence の主張と異なることを書きたいのであれば、新たに別の paragraph を作らなければならない。

(2) 結束性 (cohesion)

「結束性」とは paragraph 内の節と節、文と文の間の意味を結び付ける言語形式を指す。結束性は主に次の3つの方法により生み出される。

① 語彙の言い換えによって (lexical chain)
   Nancy → a fifteen-year-old girl → a young woman → a girl with ambition
② 代名詞や定冠詞によって (pronouns and a definite article)
   a book → the book → it

③ **つなぎ言葉によって** (transition words)
next, for example, then, first, as a result, in other words など

Exercise 10

Model Paragraph の topic sentence は、Family restaurants are popular among families for several reasons. であった。したがって、Model Paragraph の中に、例えば The last time I went to a family restaurant, I had a very good time. というような topic sentence で述べられた主張と関係のない文 (irrelevant sentence) が入っていると、paragraph の統一性 (unity) が損なわれる。さて、Model Paragraph の中には、実はもう 1 つ topic sentence で述べられた主張と関係のない文が混じっている。どの文が paragraph の統一性を乱しているだろうか。

Exercise 11

Exercise 5 で指摘したつなぎ言葉を含めて、Model Paragraph において使われているつなぎ言葉をすべて拾い出し、（　）で示しなさい。

Exercise 12

次の paragraph の下線部分に入る適切なつなぎ言葉を選んで入れなさい。

　　Last August, I did a homestay with an American family, which oriented my course of life. Until that time, I had always been afraid to speak English in front of native speakers. (¹　　　), I missed many opportunities for good English conversation practice, (²　　　) my English speaking ability never progressed to a level appropriate for someone who had been studying for six years. (³　　　), I think my host family realized this and tried to create a stress-free environment full of interesting things in order to motivate me to speak. That visit helped me to overcome my hesitancy to use English out of fear of making a mistake. (⁴　　　), I learned that self-awareness actually helps me to pay attention to my speech, which also helps to decrease the number of errors. (⁵　　　), I have greatly improved my speaking ability. Now I actively seek situations where I can talk to native English speakers.

> moreover, however, therefore, and, thus, because

On Your Own

（1）　Exercise 4 の 1 と 2 で書き直した topic sentence のどちらか 1 つを使って、まとまりのある paragraph を書きなさい。
（2）　自分のこれまでの英語学習を振り返って、記憶に残るような出来事を Exercise 12 を参考にしてまとまりのある paragraph を書きなさい。

Vocabulary — Vocabulary Building 2

Exercise 13

次の空所に入る最も適切な語を書きなさい。イタリック体で示されている部分の表す意味が、空所に入る語の接頭辞 (prefix) の意味となっている。なお、複数形にすべき箇所にも注意しなさい。また、各語の prefix に下線を引きなさい。

1a. (　　　　) is the time in history *before* anything was written down.
1b. A message written at the end of a letter *after* you have signed your name is called a (　　　　) and often abbreviated as *p.s.*
2a. A (　　　　) is a long speech by *one* person.
2b. A (　　　　) word, such as "distribution", has *many* syllables.
3a. *Jimakusūpā* in Japanese comes from an English word (　　　　), which means putting one picture, image, or photograph *on top* of another so that both can be partly seen.
3b. A railway system that runs *under* the ground is called a (　　　　) in American English.

(*Longman Dictionary of Contemporary English*, 2003 を参考)

Exercise 14

接尾辞 (suffix) には語の末尾について元の語の品詞を変える機能を持っているものがある。

A. 次の動詞で示される「行為」を行う人、また名詞で示される「もの」を扱う人を英語で表しなさい。
　1. 動詞：① instruct (　　　) ② analyze (　　　) ③ employ (　　　)
　2. 名詞：① science (　　　) ② library (　　　) ③ engine (　　　)

B. 次の語に接尾辞を加え、指定された品詞に変えなさい。
　1. 動詞から名詞に：　① describe (　　　) ② achieve (　　　)
　2. 形容詞から名詞に：① clever (　　　) ② possible (　　　)
　3. 動詞から形容詞に：① desire (　　　) ② forget (　　　)
　4. 名詞から形容詞に：① week (　　　) ② comfort (　　　)
　5. 名詞から動詞に：　① drama (　　　) ② strength (　　　)
　6. 形容詞から動詞に：① simple (　　　) ② dark (　　　)

Chapter 6　Essay

Paragraph から essay へと視点を広げ、essay の書き方を学ぼう

パラグラフについて学んだことを基礎に、**複数の paragraph から成る essay** について考えてみよう。

Task 1

次の文章と Chapter 5 の Model Paragraph (p. 28) を比較し、どこが似ているか、またどこが異なっているかを考えなさい。

Family Restaurants

　　With developments in the economy, Japanese lifestyles, especially eating habits, have changed. A half century ago, few families could afford to eat out, but today the restaurant industry is one of the big businesses which earmark the Japanese economy. Indeed, the total revenue in this business field amounted to approximately 14 trillion in 2021. Among several types of restaurants available in Japan, the most popular type is family restaurants. There are several reasons why family restaurants are popular with families: convenience, large spaces, and the variety on the menus.

　　First of all, they are convenient. Many of them are open till late at night and all year round, so it is easy to go there whenever we want. We can even have a meal at midnight or on New Year's Day. In addition, they are located in easily accessible places. Some restaurants are located near a train station, while others are on a highway equipped with a large parking space. Therefore, going there on foot or by car for a family with small children or elderly members is not a problem.

　　Second, family restaurants are typically more spacious than other types of restaurants. This helps to reduce the waiting time or probability of not being able to get a reservation for your choice of date or time. They have a large space with many tables; therefore, families can go to such restaurants with the assurance that they can always get a table any day or time.

　　Finally, their popularity among families lies in the variety on the menus. Many types of dishes and set courses can be ordered from a wide selection of dishes besides Japanese food, such as Chinese, Italian or American. Thus, we can choose our favorite dishes. In addition, the wide assortment of dishes on the menu allows for choice in how much the family spends on their meal. The dishes and courses offered are usually reasonably priced. For example, at some restaurants there are several dishes which cost less than eight hundred yen. There are also special set courses, which include a salad, soup, a main dish, rice or bread, and dessert with coffee or tea. Therefore, families can enjoy their meals whether they want a budget meal or a higher-priced one.

In conclusion, families often choose family-style restaurants when dining out because their opening hours and locations are convenient, they have large spaces with a lot of tables, and their menus include various choices and prices. These days family restaurants are an indispensable part of Japanese families' typical way of life. Thus, the demand for this type of restaurant will probably never go down.

1. 「エッセイ」と "essay" の違い

何よりもまず注意したい点は、日本語の「エッセイ」と英語の "essay" とはまったく違うという点である。辞書ではおのおの次のように定義されていて、日英の定義は大きく異なっている。

エッセイ：　自由な形式で作者の感想や意見を綴ったもの（『図解外来語辞典』1987）
Essay：　　a short literary composition on a particular theme or subject, usually in prose and generally analytic, speculative, or interpretative. (*The Random House Dictionary of the English Language,* 1987)（下線は筆者による）

このように英語の essay は、作者の「感想」を思いつくまま「自由に」、「私は...と感じました」というようなスタイルで書く「感想文」とはまったく異質のもので、「分析的に」作者の「論旨」を「説明」したものでなくてはならない。

2. 英語の essay の特徴

Task 2

次の①～⑤は、異なる母語を持つ学生が書いた英作文に見られた論理構造を印象的に図式化したものである。①から⑤で示されたものが、イ～ホのどの言語を母語とする学生によって書かれたものか考えてみよう。

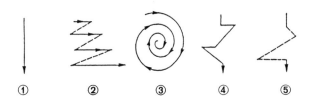

（Kaplan, 1966 より）

イ．日本語　　ロ．ロシア語　　ハ．アラビア語　　ニ．英語　　ホ．フランス語

3. Essay の構成

Essay は paragraph 同様、3つの主要部分から成っている。
(1) **Introductory Paragraph**（序論）
(2) **Body Paragraphs**（本論）
(3) **Concluding Paragraph**（結論）

基本的に、essay の構成は、paragraph の構成を拡大したものとして考えることができる。paragraph と essay の対応は図1のようになっている。

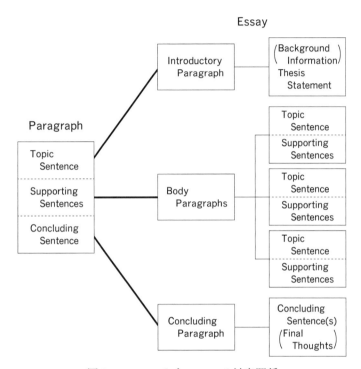

図1　paragraph と essay の対応関係

(1) Introductory Paragraph（序論）の役割
① 読者の関心を引く。
② 主張に関しての**背景知識**を読者に与える。
③ **Essay 全体の筆者の主張**を示す。
④ Essay がどのような構成になっているのかを予告する（Preview）こともある。

上記の①〜④について、さらに詳しく解説すると...
① Introductory paragraph は上記①で記した役割を果たすために、通常、背景知識を与えるための概略的な情報から始まり、次第に論旨に結びつくよう essay の焦点を絞り込み、最後に thesis statement（主題文）で主張を明示するという形式をとる。（図2参照）
② 概略的な情報を与える部分では、論旨に関する背景知識を与える。ここでは、事実

や統計的数字を示したり、歴史上のエピソードを盛り込んだりすることで読者の関心を引く。
③ 次いで、essay の論旨に直接関連する情報を与える。
④ Thesis statement は paragraph の topic sentence に当たるもので、essay 全体の論旨を示す部分である。
⑤ Thesis statement は essay 全体の構造と次に続く body paragraphs の内容を予告することもある。

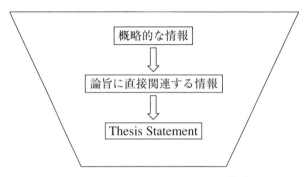

図 2　Introductory Paragraph の構造

Exercise 1

Model Essay の introductory paragraph を以下の点から分析しなさい。

(1) 図 2 を参照し、1) 概略的な背景知識を与えている部分に下線を、論旨に直接関連する情報に二重線を、thesis statement に波線を引きなさい。

(2) Model Essay はいくつの body paragraphs から成り立っていると予想されますか。また、それぞれの body paragraph は何について述べられていると予想されますか。

Exercise 2

次の文を並べ替えて、introductory paragraph を作りなさい。また、それぞれの introductory paragraph には、読者の関心を引くために、どのような手法が使われているかを考えなさい。

(1) ① Today, however, nuclear families are common not only in urban areas but also in rural areas.
② In pre-war Japan, seven out of ten families were extended families.
③ There are several differences in lifestyles between extended and nuclear families.
④ Styles of families have been rapidly changing.
　(　) → (　) → (　) → (　)

(2) ① The story of a dog named Hachi, which was kept by a professor of Tokyo Imperial University Hidesaburo Ueno, is well known to many Japanese.
② Keeping dogs has been common in Japan for a long time.
③ There are several reasons why dogs are well loved by Japanese.
④ Besides Hachi, there are other famous dogs in Japan, such as Kinako, a dog which became a police dog by overcoming a series of difficulties.
(　) → (　) → (　) → (　)

(2) Body paragraphs (本論)
① Body paragraphs は主題で明らかにした論旨を展開する部分である。
② いくつの paragraph を書くかは論旨によって異なる。
③ それぞれの body paragraph は topic sentence, supporting sentences, detail(s) から成る。

Exercise 3
Model Essay の body paragraphs について以下の問いに答えなさい。
(1) Model Essay はいくつの body paragraphs から成り立っていますか。
(2) それぞれの body paragraph の topic sentence に下線を引きなさい。

(3) Concluding Paragraph (結論)
Concluding paragraph は、読者に強い印象を与えながら essay を締めくくるという重要な役割を担っている。Paragraph の concluding sentence の場合同様、以下の点に注意して書く必要がある。
① Thesis statement で述べた論旨を別の言葉で言い換える。
② 文章全体の内容を要約する。
③ **In conclusion, In summary** などのつなぎ言葉で導入されることが多い。
④ さらに余韻を残すために予測、提案などの final thought(s) を付け加える場合もあるが、この要素は必ずしも必要なものではない。

Exercise 4
以下に示した Model Essay の concluding paragraph について答えなさい。
(1) Model Essay の thesis statement は次のようなものでした。

> There are several reasons why family restaurants are popular with families: convenience, large spaces, and the variety on the menus.

この thesis statement を構成する各要素は、concluding paragraph の中の concluding sentence ではどのように言い換えられていますか。

① family restaurants are popular with families → _____
② convenience → _____
③ large spaces → _____
④ the variety on the menus → _____

(2) Concluding paragraph はどのようなつなぎ言葉によって導入されていますか。

(3) Final thought の部分を（ ）でくくりなさい。

4. アウトラインの書き方

アウトラインは、**文章全体の要点をまとめる**上で大変重要なものである。アウトラインのそれぞれの項目は、**短い文や語句**で表すことが多い。アウトラインは以下の様式で作られるが、見出しとして使われる**文字や数字の使い分け**に注意しよう。

```
                    タイトル
   I. （ローマ数字）  Thesis Statement
  II. Body Paragraph 1 の Topic Sentence
       A. （アルファベットの大文字） Supporting Sentence 1
            1. （アラビア数字） Supporting Sentence 1 の Detail 1
            2. Supporting Sentence 1 の Detail 2
       B. Supporting Sentence 2
            1. Supporting Sentence 2 の Detail 1
            2. Supporting Sentence 2 の Detail 2
 III. Body Paragraph 2 の Topic Sentence
  IV. Body Paragraph 3 の Topic Sentence
   V. Concluding Sentence(s)
```

Exercise 5

Model Essay のアウトラインを完成しなさい。（ ）には 1 語、_____ には 1 語以上を入れなさい。

```
                 Family Restaurants
   I. There are several (1     ) why (2     ) (3         ) are popular with families
  II. Convenient
       A. (4     ) till late at night and all year round
            1. Can have a meal at (5     )
            2. Can have a meal on (6     ) (7     ) (8     )
       B. Located in easily (9     ) places.
            1. Near a (10     ) (11     ) (can go on foot)
            2. On a (12     ) (can go by car)
```

III. More (^{13})
   A. Can reduce the (^{14}) (^{15})
   B. Can reduce the (^{16}) of not being able to get a reservation

IV. ^{17} _____
   A. ^{18} _____
      1. Japanese food
      2. ^{19} _____
      3. ^{20} _____
      4. ^{21} _____
   B. ^{22} _____
      1. Dishes that cost less than ^{23} _____
      2. Special ^{24} _____

V. ^{25} _____

Exercise 6

次のおのおのの主題文に最も適した結論文を選びなさい。

1. I prefer studying at an American university to studying at a Japanese university.
   a. In my opinion, American universities are better than universities in other countries.
   b. In conclusion, I prefer studying at an American university to studying at a Japanese university.
   c. In short, I would rather pursue my studies at a university in the States than in Japan.
2. Computer games are not always beneficial for children because too much time spent playing these games affects their schoolwork, eyes, and personality.
   a. In conclusion, computer games are not always good playthings, so they can affect children's studies, eyes, and personality.
   b. In conclusion, parents should not let their children play computer games because these games damage children's physical as well as mental health.
   c. In conclusion, computer games can be harmful for children because overuse of these games tends to make children neglect their schoolwork, have bad eyesight, and have trouble getting along with other children.

Exercise 7

次の文章は essay についてまとめたものである。これまでに学んだことから考えて、( ) の中に適語を下から選んで入れなさい。

　　An English essay has a (1　　) structure consisting of (2　　) major parts. The first part is an (3　　) paragraph with a (4　　) statement which shows the main idea of the whole essay. The functions of this first part are to attract readers' (5　　), to give background (6　　) to the readers, and to indicate the general organization. The second part is (7　　) paragraphs, which develop the main idea presented in the first part. The last part is a (8　　) paragraph. The functions of this part are to (9　　) the major points and to (10　　) the main idea expressed in the thesis statement.

> summarize, attention, thesis, concluding, information, restate, topic, linear, three, body, essay, middle, introductory, ending, circular

On Your Own

Exercise 6 の中の 1 か 2 のいずれかを選び、与えられている主題文及び結論文を使って、エッセイを書きなさい。

Vocabulary — つなぎ言葉

Chapter 5 でも触れたが、つなぎ言葉 (transition words) は文と文、あるいは節と節を結びつけ、文章全体にスムースな流れをつくるものである。また、読者を混乱することなく、導く道しるべの役割もはたしている。つなぎ言葉の種類としては副詞(句)と等位及び従属接続詞がある。主なつなぎ言葉を機能別にまとめると次のようになる。

機能	副詞(句)	接続詞 等位	接続詞 従属
補 足	furthermore, moreover / in addition	and	
対 比	however / on the other hand	but / yet	though / although
類 似	similarly, likewise	and	while
選 択	otherwise	or	
結 果	therefore, consequently / as a result	so	

理　由		for	because
例　示	for example, for instance		
経過・順序	then, next, finally		
	first, second,		
言い換え	that is, in other words		
結　論	in conclusion, in summary,		
	in brief		

あわせて、句読点の使い方にも気をつけよう。
(1) 副詞（句）の場合
　　A. 節; 副詞(句), 節　〔例〕Tom is an only child; however, he is not spoiled.
　　B. 文. 副詞(句), 文　〔例〕Tom is an only child. However, he is not spoiled.
(2) 等位接続詞の場合：節, 等位接続詞＋節
　　〔例〕Tom is an only child, but he is not spoiled.
(3) 従属接続詞の場合：節＋従属接続詞＋節
　　〔例〕Tom is not spoiled though he is an only child.
　　ただし、Though Tom is an only child, he is not spoiled.（従属節が主節の前に置かれた時はカンマをつける）

Exercise 8

次の文章を読み、適切なつなぎ言葉を下から選んで空所に入れなさい。

　　While each cultural group is equipped with a variety of arts ranging from fine arts to literature, it seems that each culture has stressed and developed a particular variety. France, (1　　　), is known for paintings, (2　　　) Paris is said to be the center of fine arts. (3　　　), Italy has famous painters and sculptors such as Botticelli and Michelangelo. (4　　　), Germany is famous for classical music. Many outstanding composers are of German origin: Bach, Beethoven, and Wagner. (5　　　), Russia has literature as its representative variety of art. Long novels by Tolstoy and Dostoevski are real masterpieces known throughout the world. (6　　　), (7　　　) every cultural group has several different branches of art, each has developed its own distinctive branch in history.

---

for example,　furthermore,　in conclusion,　and,　finally,　though,　similarly

Chapter 7　Process

ひと続きの行為のプロセスを順序立て、段階を追って説明してみよう

この章では**ある一連の行為の過程を説明する**文章の書き方を学ぶ。時間の流れに沿って書かれる文章であり、したがって、narration で学んだ**時を表す語句**を再度復習する必要がある。それに加えて**順序を示す語句**を使いこなす必要もある。

Task 1

次の例文は、アメリカでの結婚式が行われるまでの過程を説明した文章である。この例文を読み、順序を示している表現に下線を引きなさい。最初の2つの表現にはすでに下線を引いてある。

An American Wedding

　　In America, weddings are usually planned by the bride-to-be and her groom. It is a procedure which takes a lot of time, and usually these preparations are begun one year before the wedding. There are many things a couple needs to consider when planning a wedding.

5　　The first thing to consider is the date. The couple must not only choose a date that is special for them, but they must also consider the schedules of their guests. In addition, there will be many details that need their involvement, so the couple will need to allow themselves enough time for preparation. Thus, the date should be chosen with these things in mind.

10　　The next biggest consideration is the style of the wedding ceremony and the reception that follows. Choosing a style will also influence the location. The ceremony can be a formal or semi-formal event, such as an evening candlelight service or one in the afternoon. Traditionally, these kinds of ceremonies are held in a church. On the other hand, it can be a small casual event at home or somewhere outside such
15　as in a park or even on top of a mountain. Next, the couple must decide the type of reception they want. It usually follows the ceremony and is held nearby. Receptions usually range from a simple buffet to a sit-down dinner with dancing and a live band.

　　The last things to decide are the details of the ceremony and related wedding events. This is the busiest time. First, the guest list and registry must be discussed.
20　Next, the theme colors must be chosen. These colors will be used later when deciding

items such as the invitation, the thank you card, the bridesmaids' and groomsmen's apparel, flowers and decorations. Picking out the cake, music and visual presentation or pamphlet about themselves are also things traditionally done by the couple as some of the final steps.

In sum, a wedding is a marvelous event with lasting memories, especially if planned carefully and lovingly by the bride-to-be and her groom. This is the first step in preparation for the rest of their lives.

Task 2

次の各文をよく読み、"An American Wedding"の内容と一致するように、正しい順序に並べ換えなさい。

(a) The type of reception needs to be chosen.
(b) A couple must choose a date for their wedding.
(c) The couple have to think about the cake, music, and visual presentation or pamphlet about themselves.
(d) The couple have to consider the style of the wedding ceremony.
(e) The theme color must be decided.
(f) The couple must discuss the guest list and registry.
(　) → (　) → (　) → (　) → (　) → (　)

Task 3

次の各文をよく読み、筋が通るように、正しい順序に並べ換えなさい。

(a) Yoko found a book on the topic.
(b) Yoko went to the library to find some information.
(c) Yoko checked the book out.
(d) Yoko wrote down the title of the book.
(e) Yoko brought the book home.
(f) Yoko had to write a paper on global warming.
(g) Yoko went to the section where the book was supposed to be located.
(h) Yoko used a computer database at the library.
(i) Yoko found the book.
(j) Yoko wrote down the call number of the book.
(k) Yoko took the book from the shelf.
(　) → (　) → (　) → (　) → (　) → (　) → (　) → (　) → (　) → (　) → (　)

Rhetoric — 各ステップの順序を明確にし、スムースな流れを作る

各ステップの順序を明確にし、スムースな流れを作るには、ある行為の各ステップの順序を明確にし、また各ステップをスムースに流れるように結びつける必要がある。このためには、以下の3点に気をつけなければならない。

(1) 時を表す表現や順序を表すつなぎ言葉を使うこと。
(2) 短く、細切れの文をつなげて、流れのある文にすること。
(3) 同じ語句が何回も現れるとくどくなるので、適当な代名詞で置き換えること。

例えば、Task 3を正しい順序に並べ換えてパラグラフの形にまとめると次のようになる。

Example Paragraph

① Yoko had to write a paper on global warming, so she went to the library to find some information. ② First, she used the computer database at the library and found a book on the topic. ③ She then wrote down its title and call number. ④ Next, she went to the section where it was supposed to be located. ⑤ After she found it, she took it from the shelf. ⑥ She checked it out and finally brought it home.

Exercise 1

Example Paragraph を以下の点から分析しなさい。

1. つなぎ言葉に下線を引きなさい。その中で「順序」を表すものはどれですか。
2. 以下の（ア）〜（コ）は Task 3 で示した (a)〜(j) を時間の流れに沿って並べ替えたものである。（ア）〜（コ）のうちのどの文とどの文が結び付けられて、Example Paragraph の①〜⑤の各文に書き換えられていますか。

　　　　例：（ア）と（イ）→ ① に

(ア)　Yoko had to write a paper on global warming.
(イ)　Yoko went to the library to find some information.
(ウ)　Yoko used the computer database at the library.
(エ)　Yoko found a book on the topic.
(オ)　Yoko wrote down the title of the book.
(カ)　Yoko wrote down the call number of the book.
(キ)　Yoko went to the section where the book was supposed to be located.
(ク)　Yoko found the book.
(ケ)　Yoko took the book from the shelf.
(コ)　Yoko checked the book out.
(サ)　Yoko brought the book home.

3. 上の（ア）〜（コ）の中のどの語句が、Example Paragraph ではどのような代名詞に言い換えられていますか。

　　　　例：（イ）の Yoko → ① の she

Chapter 7　Process　47

Exercise 2

次の各文をよく読み、筋が通るように、正しい順序に並べ換えなさい。
(a)　Taro inserted his cash card.
(b)　Taro did not have enough money on hand.
(c)　Taro found a cash dispenser.
(d)　Taro pushed several other buttons to show the amount of money he wanted.
(e)　Taro got some money in cash.
(f)　Taro went to the bank.
(g)　Taro pushed the button marked "Withdraw."
(h)　Taro wanted to buy a new suit.
(i)　The machine told Taro to wait for a minute.
(j)　Taro pushed his PIN.

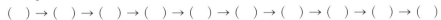

Exercise 3

Task 2 と Exercise 2 で正しい順序に並べ換えた各文を、Rhetoric で述べた (1)〜(3) の手法を使って、パラグラフの形にまとめなさい。

Exercise 4

次の 1〜10 はフレンチ・トーストの作り方を示したものです。おのおのの絵をよく見て、与えられた動詞を使って、各ステップを 1 文で表現してみなさい。材料の分量や調理器具も明示しなさい。

1. Beat . . .
2. Stir in . . .
3. Place . . .
4. Cover . . .
5. Dip . . .
6. Fry . . .
7. Turn . . .
8. Brown . . .
9. Serve . . .
10. Add . . .

Exercise 5

Exercise 4 で書いた 10 の文を、Rhetoric で学んだ 3 つの手法を使って、パラグラフの形にまとめなさい。

Exercise 6

次の地図で矢印で示したものは Ocean Station からフランス料理店である Paris House までの道順です。

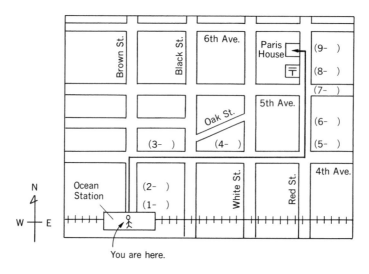

次の a～i の各文をよく読み、おのおのの文が地図で示したどの部分に当たるのかを考え、地図上の（ ）にその記号を記しなさい。（例：1-g）

a. Turn right at the first intersection.
b. Cross Fifth Avenue.
c. Go past the post office.
d. Go along Fourth Avenue for about three blocks until you come to Red Street.
e. Turn left on Red Street.

f. Paris House is on the left side.
g. Go out of the north exit of Ocean Station.
h. Go straight on Brown Street.
i. Walk one block on Red Street.

Exercise 7

Rhetoric で学んだ3つの手法を復習し，上記の Exercise 6 で並べ換えた文をまとまった文章として書き換えなさい。ただし，最初の2文と最後の1文は与えられています。

We are going to have a Christmas party at a French restaurant called Paris House. It is easy to get to Paris House from Ocean Station. _____

_____

_____ You can't miss it!

On Your Own

(1) 日本を初めて訪れる外国人に対して、わかりやすく温泉の入り方について説明しなさい。
(2) 日本食のうちの一品を取り上げ、日本を初めて訪れる外国人に対してわかりやすく、その作り方を説明しなさい。
(3) あなたの推薦するレストランへの行き方を、レストランの最寄り駅を始点として説明しなさい。また、その店のお勧め料理や雰囲気など推薦する理由もつけ加えなさい。

Vocabulary — 料理動詞

この chapter で調理法の書き方（recipe writing）をしてみて、日本語と英語の料理動詞の選択が難しいと思った人も多かったかもしれない。料理法というのはそれぞれの国や生活様式に深く根ざしているので、料理動詞の意味範囲も文化によって変わってくる。

Task 4

次の表を見てそれぞれの動詞がどのような基準で分類されているか、日本語と対応させて考えてみよう。英語の動詞で意味の不明なものがあったら、辞書で調べてみよう。

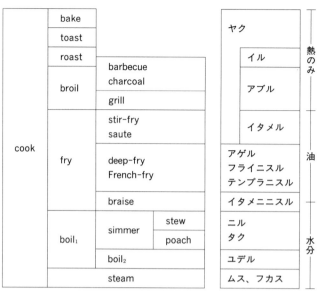

(國廣、1981 より)

日本語については省略するとして、英語の料理動詞について見てみよう。肉が食事の中心となる欧米では、肉や卵の料理法に関する語彙が豊富であることに気づく。どのように加熱するのか、また何を加熱するのかによってさまざまな動詞が選ばれる。

Task 5

日本語の「焼く」という動詞に対し、英語では bake, toast, roast という 3 つの動詞を当てている。それぞれの加熱の仕方や、焼く対象物はどのようなものであるか考えなさい。

	加熱法	対象物
bake		
roast		
toast		

この他、注意すべき動詞を取り上げてみる。

英語の fry については日本語の「アゲル」が一番近いが、ヤク・イタメルにも対応している。例えば、「卵焼き」は fried egg である。stir-fry というのは中国料理でよく用いる炒め方である。deep-fry はてんぷらのように深い鍋で揚げるものである。french-fry は deep-fry と調理法は同じであるが、対象物が french-fry の場合、french-fried potatoes（フライド・ポテト）に代表されるように、細長く切ったものを揚げるときに使う。

braise はフライパンなどで少し油をひいて炒めたのち、何かソースのような液体を加えてさらに煮る場合に用いる。「照り焼きチキン」などはこれにあたる。

boil₁ と boil₂ の区別は、後者が沸点以上の湯などの液体でぐらぐらと煮えたぎるのを指すのに対し、前者は沸点以下で加熱する意味の simmer をも含む大きな意味での動詞である。

Chapter 8　Definition

ことばを定義づけるタイプの文章を学ぼう

この章ではものごとや概念を定義する文章の書き方を学ぶ。

Task

次の文章を読んで、問題の下線部を完成させなさい。

A Good Language Learner

　　Being a "good language learner" is not equal to being a nice, polite student. A "good" learner is not defined by a person's outward personality. Actually, the definition of a "good language learner" is a student who has the qualities of motivation, a readiness to take risks, and determination to apply language skills outside of the classroom.

　　The first quality, motivation, is possibly the most important. A motivated language learner is a person with strong interests or reasons which give him or her the determination to find his or her own way to use the language. Finding one's own way may include organizing information about the language, such as rhymes or word associations to remember what has been learned. Motivation to use the language may inspire creativity. For example, the learner may experiment with various ways to keep a conversation going.

　　The second characteristic of a good language learner is a readiness to take risks. It is said that learners learn from their mistakes. They do not mind uncertainty and develop strategies for making sense of the language without feeling the need to understand every word. They learn to make intelligent guesses.

　　Finally, good language learners are those who seek opportunities to practice outside of the classroom. For example, they may visit countries where that language is spoken, listen to songs of that country, sing, or read for pleasure in that language. Much of their free time may be spent watching television or videos in which the people speak only the language they are studying.

　　In conclusion, being a "good language learner" is not related to one's personality; rather it means being motivated, ready to take risks and determined to become "good" at using the language.

(Adapted from: Rubin, 1975)

この文章全体の主題文 (thesis statement)：

_____

第 2 paragraph で述べられている "a good language learner" の定義：

_____

例 1：_____
例 2：_____

第 3 paragraph で述べられている "a good language learner" の定義：

_____

例 1：_____
例 2：_____

第 4 paragraph で述べられている "a good language learner" の定義：

_____

例 1：_____
例 2：_____

Rhetoric 1 — Definition（定義づけ）

　話し言葉では、ある言葉がどういう意味かを説明したいとき、次のように言うことがある。「僕の弟の次郎はとても自分勝手な人間なんだ」そして、「自分勝手」という言葉を説明するために続けて、「次郎は自分のゲーム機を貸してくれないんだ」というように言う。一方、書き言葉では、ある言葉をどういう意味で使っているのかということを、もう少し改まった形で次のように表す。

(1) 一文で定義する場合

文は次のように組み立てられる。

$$言葉 = \underline{カテゴリー（範疇）} + \begin{Bmatrix} 関係代名詞 \\ 関係副詞 \end{Bmatrix} + \underline{特徴}$$

　カテゴリー（範疇）というのはその言葉が属している分野のことであり、特徴というのはそのほかの言葉と区別される目立った特徴のことである。下の例で見てみよう。

具体的な物の場合:

- Onigiri is <u>a Japanese food</u> <u>which is made with rice rolled into a ball and covered with seaweed</u>.
  （カテゴリー）　　　　　　　　　　　（特徴）

- Tempura is <u>a Japanese food</u> <u>which is made with fish and vegetables dipped in batter and deep-fat fried</u>.
  （カテゴリー）　　　　　　　　　　　（特徴）

抽象的な概念の場合:
- An optimist is <u>a person</u> <u>who looks at things positively</u>.
  （カテゴリー）　　（特徴）

- A pessimist is <u>a person</u> <u>who looks at things negatively</u>.
  （カテゴリー）　　（特徴）

(2) 文章で定義する場合（Extended definiton）：

ある1つのことを定義する場合、1つの文では定義づけができないことがしばしばある。また、ものによっては複数の paragraph を必要とすることもある。

「お正月」を例に取って考えてみよう。次の手順を踏んで文章が組み立てられる。

1. 「お正月」が属しているカテゴリーは何か。

    Oshogatsu is a holiday.

    もっと詳しく言うと、*Oshogatsu* is a holiday with many traditions.

2. ほかの祝日と区別される特色は何か。

    It commemorates the New Year in Japan.

3. その他の特色は何か。

    There are special food, decorations, and greetings for *oshogatsu*.

これらをまとめると次のような文章が出来上がる。

Oshogatsu is the holiday which commemorates the New Year in Japan. The holiday is celebrated with special traditions that are seen in the food, decorations, and greetings.

Exercise 1

次の主題文や特徴を利用して「お正月」を定義する文章を完成させなさい。

> There are more traditions associated with *oshogatsu* than any other period of days on the Japanese calendar. *Oshogatsu* is the holiday which commemorates the New Year in Japan. The holiday is celebrated with special traditions that are seen in the food, decorations, and greetings.

> Special food is eaten on this day and the following six days. . . .

> In addition to the special food, there are special decorations. . . .

> Among traditions for the New Year is the custom for people to pay their first visit of the year to a shrine or temple. This greeting is called . . .

In conclusion, ...

Rhetoric 2 — 関係代名詞

関係代名詞はほとんどの場合、名詞を修飾する形容詞節を作るために使われる。用法には限定的用法と継続的用法がある。

　　限定的用法： Leonardo da Vinci was the artist who painted the Mona Lisa.
　　　　　　　　　　　　　　　　　　先行詞　　関係代名詞節(＝形容詞節)
　　（関係詞節が形容詞節となって先行詞を修飾し、その意味を限定している。）
　　継続的用法： His mother, who has been ill, is better now.
　　（先行詞の意味を限定しているのではなく、単に余分の説明を加えているだけのものでコンマで区切られる。）
使い方は次のように分けられる。

先行詞＼格	主　格	所有格	目的格
人	who, that	whose	who(m), that
物	which, that	whose, of which	which, that

Rhetoric 3 — 関係副詞

関係副詞は「前置詞＋関係代名詞」の役割を持っている。

(1) I was born in the year when human beings landed on the moon for the first time.
　　　　　　　　　　　　　　(in which)
(2) This is the town where my father was born.
　　　　　　　　　　　(in which)
(3) Tell me the reason why you don't want to do the job.
　　　　　　　　　　　　(for which)
(4) This is how I discovered his secret.
　　(the way in which)

Exercise 2

次の2つの文を関係詞を使って1つの文にしなさい。

1. Dogs are trained at the Sight Foundation. They help the visually impaired people to lead active lives.

2. The woman was wearing a red sweater. She used to be a model.

3. The photograph shows two women on bicycles. The detective took the photograph.

4. I was born in Utah. There is a saltwater lake in Utah.

Exercise 3

次の単語の定義を説明するような文を作りなさい。その際、例のように、与えられた単語を修飾する関係詞節を作って書きなさい。

例： school (a place)： A school is <u>a place where people study</u>.
(1) koala (an animal)： _____
(2) clown (a person)： _____
(3) soccer (a sport)： _____
(4) December 25th (the day)： _____
(5) morning (the time)： _____
(6) refugee (a person whose を使って)： _____

Rhetoric 4 ― 従属接続詞

who や which などの関係代名詞は形容詞節を作ったが、since や if などの従属接続詞と呼ばれるものは副詞節を作る。副詞節は主節の動詞が示す行為が how「どのように」、when「いつ」、where「どこで」、why「なぜ」、to what extent (how much or how long)「どの程度」、under what condition「どういう条件のもとで」行われているか (行われたか) などという問いに答えるものである。

〔例〕 The cat moves <u>as if it were afraid</u>.
　　　(「どのように猫が動いているか」に答えている)
　　There was a loud scream <u>when the lights went out</u>.
　　　(「いつ大きな悲鳴がしたか」に答えている)
　　We stood <u>where we could see the singer</u>.
　　　(「どこに立っていたか」に答えている)
　　<u>Because the temperature was very low</u>, the water froze.
　　　(「なぜ水が凍ったか」に答えている)
　　We worked <u>until we were finished</u>.
　　　(「いつまで仕事をしていたか」に答えている)
　　<u>If it is sunny tomorrow</u>, we will go to the beach.
　　　(「どのような条件のもとで海辺に行くか」に答えている)

従属接続詞には次のようなものある。

*after	as soon as	so that	whenever
although	because	than	where
as	*before	though	wherever
as if	if	unless	whether
as though	in order that	*until	while
as long as	*since	when	

（＊のついたものは前置詞としても使われる）

Exercise 4

次の1〜6に適切な副詞節をつけ加えなさい。

1. The cat meowed.

2. Our team won.

3. Lori speaks French.

4. Bob wants to be a teacher.

5. I was almost asleep.

6. John finished his homework early.

On Your Own

次の言葉を定義しなさい。（読み手は外国人であると想定しなさい）
1. お年玉　（1文で書きなさい）
2. 握り寿司　（1文で書きなさい）
3. あなたの学校：＿＿＿＿＿＿＿大学　（文章で書きなさい）
4. 本音と建前　（文章で書きなさい）

Vocabulary — アカデミックな語彙習得のために (1)

　立派な内容のessayや研究論文であっても、そこで使われている文体や語彙・表現がカジュアルなものであると、読み手によい印象を与えず、せっかくの内容の評価さえも低くなってしまう。英語のアカデミックな英文を書く際には、口語表現とは決別し、フォーマルな英文を書くようにしなくてはならない。アカデミックな英文とはどのようなものを指すのか、語彙、表現、文体の各面から検討してみよう。

① 動　詞

　アカデミックな文章というと、各分野により、使われる名詞が異なるのは当然であるが、使われる動詞は分野が異なっても共通するところがある。ひとつの法則として「句動詞 → ラテン語を起源とする動詞」に変換することが挙げられる。日本語の訳にも注目してみると、日本語においても研究論文にふさわしい語彙と日常的に使われている語彙とがあることに気づく。

〔例〕　**look at → observed**

Researchers looked at the results of the experiment carefully.
（研究者たちは実験の結果を注意深く見た。）
→ Researchers observed the results of the experiment carefully.
（研究者たちは実験の結果を注意深く観察した。）

Exercise 5

次の英文がアカデミックな文章になるように、下線の語句を下の選択肢の語と入れ替え、正しい形にしなさい。

1. When stress builds up, we experience certain physical or emotional stress signals.
2. Several family members helped out with child care, which allowed us to work and attend school.
3. The Government intends to set up a comprehensive health care system at the community level.
4. The risk of the disease goes up with the amount of tobacco smoked and the number of years of smoking.
5. People can cut down the risk of side effects from medication by keeping themselves informed about all drugs being taken.

　　　　increase　accumulate　establish　reduce　assist

Chapter 9　Classification
ものごとをグループに分類し、例をあげて説明してみよう

複雑なトピックを扱った essay を書く場合には、トピックを下位区分してサブ・トピックを作り、おのおののサブ・トピックについての paragraph を書く必要がある。こうした書き方は **classification**（分類）と呼ばれている。サブ・トピックはお互いに何らかの共通要素によって結びついている。

Task
次の Model Essay を読み、(1) essay 全体のトピックと、(2) 3つのサブ・トピックを明らかにしなさい。

Three Meals of the Day

　What would be considered American food? Except for the food of Native Americans, almost everything else came from other countries. Yet, we can describe an American meal and food which is typical at each meal. All three meals of the day, breakfast, lunch and dinner, are quite distinct.

5　　The first meal of the day is breakfast. It is often just a bowl of hot or cold cereal with milk. Eggs, bacon and toast are also a typical breakfast. There are many convenience foods on the market today which can quickly and easily be fixed in a toaster or eaten straight from the refrigerator. Quick and easy are the key words for breakfast foods. On a weekend morning, when people have more leisure time, or on
10　special occasions, hot pancakes and waffles are served with soft butter and maple syrup.

　　The second meal of the day is lunch, usually eaten around noon. A steaming bowl of soup and a hot or cold sandwich with fruit or cookies for dessert is typical among the young as well as the old. Many students and company employees will
15　bring their lunch in a brown paper bag. This is called "brown-bagging it." Take-out ethnic foods are also very popular, especially Mexican and Chinese.

　　The last and biggest meal of the day is dinner. Dinner is usually a hot platter of meat or fish, one starchy food such as potatoes or bread, a vegetable or two and a salad. Dessert, such as ice cream, pie or cake comes after dinner. Dinner is usually
20　eaten between five-thirty and six o'clock.

There is a saying, "You are what you eat." Just as Americans are very different in character from each other, so can individual differences be found in the three daily meals they eat.

Rhetoric — Classification

"Classify"（分類する）とは、同じような性質を持った物や事柄をグループとしてまとめることである。Classification を書くに当たっては、まず、グループ間の相違が明らかになるように、**分類の基準**を明確にしなければならない。ついで、各グループに分類された**事例**（動物、事物、人物、事柄など）を取り上げ、説明することになる。

Exercise 1

モデル・エッセイを参考にして、下記の空所を埋めなさい。

Three Meals of the Day

Basis of classification : ＿＿＿＿＿＿

I. ＿＿＿＿＿＿
  A. cereal   D. toaster items
  B. eggs   E. ＿＿＿＿＿＿
  C. bacon   F. waffles

II. ＿＿＿＿＿＿
  A. soup   D. cookies
  B. ＿＿＿＿＿＿   E. ＿＿＿＿＿＿
  C. fruit

III. ＿＿＿＿＿＿
  A. meat platter   E. vegetable
  B. fish platter   F. ＿＿＿＿＿＿
  C. potatoes   G. dessert
  D. ＿＿＿＿＿＿

Exercise 2

下記に示した食べ物を 2 つのグループに分類し、下線部を埋めなさい。

| carrot   orange   lettuce   banana   spinach   radish |

Group I : ＿＿＿＿＿＿
  A. ＿＿＿＿＿＿   C. ＿＿＿＿＿＿
  B. ＿＿＿＿＿＿   D. ＿＿＿＿＿＿
Group II : ＿＿＿＿＿＿
  A. ＿＿＿＿＿＿   B. ＿＿＿＿＿＿

Exercise 3

Exercise 2 で作った Group I をさらに下位区分した場合、どのようになりますか。下線部を埋めなさい。

　　　　　　　　Group I : ＿＿＿＿＿＿＿
　　　　　　　　　　Subgroup　A. ＿＿＿＿＿＿＿
　　　　　　　　　　　　　　　　1. ＿＿＿＿＿＿＿
　　　　　　　　　　　　　　　　2. ＿＿＿＿＿＿＿
　　　　　　　　　　Subgroup　B. ＿＿＿＿＿＿＿
　　　　　　　　　　　　　　　　1. ＿＿＿＿＿＿＿
　　　　　　　　　　　　　　　　2. ＿＿＿＿＿＿＿

Exercise 4

Exercise 3 で行った分類をもとにして、次の文を完成しなさい。

　　There are various kinds of ＿＿＿＿＿＿＿. Some kinds are ＿＿＿＿＿＿＿ and some kinds are ＿＿＿＿＿＿＿.

Exercise 5

次の語（句）はすべて建物に関するものです。これらの語（句）を下記に示した4つのグループに分類しなさい。なお、どのグループにも属さないものも含まれています。

> airport, apartment, concert hall, dental office, drugstore, factory, fire department, hospital, house, machine shop, movie theater, school, shoe store, restaurant, train station, welfare office

　　　　I.　Buildings people live in
　　　　　　A. ＿＿＿＿＿＿＿
　　　　　　B. ＿＿＿＿＿＿＿
　　　　II.　Buildings people shop in
　　　　　　A. ＿＿＿＿＿＿＿
　　　　　　B. ＿＿＿＿＿＿＿
　　　　III.　Buildings people are helped in
　　　　　　A. ＿＿＿＿＿＿＿　　　C. ＿＿＿＿＿＿＿
　　　　　　B. ＿＿＿＿＿＿＿
　　　　IV.　Buildings people are entertained in
　　　　　　A. ＿＿＿＿＿＿＿　　　C. ＿＿＿＿＿＿＿
　　　　　　B. ＿＿＿＿＿＿＿

Exercise 6

Exercise 5 で学んだ語彙を使って、次のパラグラフを完成しなさい。

(¹   ) can be classified on the basis of purpose of use. The size and shape of the building can vary according to its purpose. For example, buildings in which people live are called residential buildings. (²   ) and (³   ) are both kinds of residential buildings. (⁴   ) and (⁵   ) are sorts of buildings for shopping. (⁶   ), (⁷   ) and (⁸   ) are examples of buildings where people are helped. Lastly, buildings for entertainment come in many varieties, such as (⁹   ), (¹⁰   ), and (¹¹   ).

On Your Own

次に示した基準のどれかを用いて、さまざまなスポーツを分類した文章を書きなさい。
（1） どの季節に主に行われるか。
（2） どこで行われるか。（屋内か屋外か）
（3） 個人で行われるか、団体で行われるか。
（4） どのような器具が用いられるか。
（5） 男子中心のものか、女子中心のものか。

Vocabulary — アカデミックな語彙習得のために (2)

② 形容詞・副詞

英語の語彙の豊かさは動詞だけに限らない。形容詞や副詞も同じことである。ことにアカデミックな文章の場合、ものや事態の様子を表す形容詞・副詞ついては厳密になることが必要になってくる。あまり概念の広い語を使うのではなく、意味的に厳密でしかもフォーマルな用法の形容詞・副詞を選ぶことが大切である。

〔例〕 We made good progress in solving environmental problems.
（環境問題の解決においてよい進歩があった。）
→ We made considerable progress in solving environmental problems.
（環境問題の解決においてかなりの進歩があった。）

Exercise 7

次の英文がアカデミックな文になるように、下線部の語句を下の選択肢の語と入れ替えなさい。

1. We know that certain genetic factors and a lot of environmental factors increase the risk of developing cancer.
2. The present study showed that prevalence of dental caries was sort of higher among urban than rural children.

3. Without their nice work, the survey would not have been possible.
4. Malaria also does big indirect harm to economic development, productivity and quality of life.

> numerous   meticulous   considerable   relatively

③ 名　詞

名詞もあまりくだけた、何にでも当てはまるようなものでなく、厳密に意味の特定できる名詞を選ぶようにする。

〔例〕　His comment challenged me to try to put some real thing into this article.
（彼のコメントによってこの件に本質的なことを見出すことになった。）
→ His comment challenged me to try to put some real substance into this article.
（彼のコメントによってこの件に本質的な事象を見出すことになった。）

Exercise 8

次の英文がアカデミックな文になるように、下線部の語句を下の選択肢の語と入れ替えなさい。

1. The student council is the (1)place where (2)persons chosen in each class exchange opinions on various (3)things for discussion.
2. A microscope is a valuable (4)thing for (5)people who investigate microbes.

> instrument   representatives   topics   researchers   organization

Chapter 10　Comparison and Contrast

ものごとがどのように似ているか、また違っているか説明してみよう

2つのものごとを比べると必ず**類似点と相違点**が見つかる。この章では、類似点と相違点を整理して、わかりやすく説明する文章の書き方を学ぶ。

1. Comparison（類似点）

Task 1

次の文章はロンドンと東京の類似点について述べたものです。2つの都市がどのように似ているかを読みとり、下記の表を例に従って完成させなさい。

Model 1

London and Tokyo

　　There are several similarities between London and Tokyo. First, London is a crowded city with a large population just as Tokyo is. London is the capital of the United Kingdom. Likewise, Tokyo is the capital of Japan. Both London and Tokyo are the centers of politics, economy, and culture. London is similar to Tokyo in that both have a convenient public transportation system: trains, subways, and buses. The British Royal Family lives in the capital, and the Japanese Imperial Family lives in the capital, too. Furthermore, not only Londoners but also Tokyoites can enjoy a variety of entertainment such as movies, theaters, musicals, concerts, and exhibitions. In short, London is as international as Tokyo, with each attracting people from different countries.

Basis of comparison / City	London	Tokyo
① population	large	
② capital of …		Japan
③ center of …	politics, economy, and culture	
④ public transportation		convenient
⑤ monarch	the Royal Family	
⑥ entertainment	various	
⑦ international		yes

Rhetoric 1 — Comparison の文章とは

2つのものごとの**類似点**を述べるcomparisonの文章を書くに当たっては、まず次の事項に注意しなければならない。

1) **同じ種類**のものごとを比較する。

　Model 1 では、ロンドンと東京という「都市」を比較した。ロンドンと日本というように、一方は「都市」、他方は「国」という異なる種類に属するものごとを比較することはできない。

2) **同一の基準**でものごとを比較する。

　Model 1 では、ロンドンと東京を比較するに当たって、第1に「人口」という物差しを使った。一方の都市を「人口」で、他方の都市を「面積」でというように異なる基準で比較することはできない。

Rhetoric 2 — Comparison にまつわる表現

Comparison の文章を書く際に鍵となる表現を学習しよう。Model 1 で用いられていた表現は波線で示されているので確認しよう。

1) 文と文を結びつけるもの：likewise, similarly, also

- London is the capital of the United Kingdom. $\left\{\begin{array}{l}\text{Likewise,}\\ \text{Similarly,}\\ \text{Also,}\end{array}\right\}$ Tokyo is the capital of Japan.

2) 節と節を結びつけるもの：just as, and ... too ...

- London is a crowded city with a large population just as Tokyo is.
- The British Royal Family lives in the capital, and the Japanese Imperial Family lives in the capital, too.

3) その他：similar to, just like, the same as, as ... as

- London is $\left\{\begin{array}{l}\text{similar to}\\ \text{just like}\\ \text{the same as}\end{array}\right\}$ Tokyo in that they both have a convenient public transportation system: trains, subways, and buses.
- London is as international as Tokyo.

4) 呼応表現：both ... and, not only ... but (also) ..., neither ... nor ...

- Both London and Tokyo are the centers of politics, economy, and culture.
- Not only Londoners but also Tokyoites can enjoy a variety of entertainment such as movies, theaters, musicals, concerts, and exhibitions.
- Neither New York nor São Paulo is a capital.

Exercise 1

次の文章をよく読み、（　）内に適切な語を入れなさい。

New York and Paris

New York and Paris have several things in common. (¹　　　) New York and Paris (²　　　) international cities where people of different nationalities live. New York is a big city in North America, just (³　　　) Paris is in Europe. New York has many tourist attractions, such as the Empire State Building and the Statue of Liberty. (⁴　　　), Paris has such famous spots as the Eiffel Tower and Notre Dame. New York has an efficient subway system, and Paris does, (⁵　　　). With this system, (⁶　　　) New Yorkers (⁷　　　) Parisians have much difficulty going from one place to another in the cities. Though the two cities are attractive as such, unfortunately, (⁸　　　) cities have another thing in (⁹　　　): New York is (¹⁰　　　) dangerous (¹¹　　　) Paris, with a high crime rate.

2. Contrast（相違点）

Task 2

次の文章はアメリカのコミュニケーション学者である Dean Barnlund が指摘したアメリカ人と日本人のコミュニケーション・スタイルにおける相違点をまとめたものです。アメリカ人と日本人がどのように異なっているかを考え、例に従って両者の相違点を列挙しなさい。

Model 2

Communication Styles of Americans and Japanese 🔊 11

　　According to an American communication researcher in the 1980s, Dr. Dean Barnlund, there are striking differences in communicative styles between Americans and Japanese. First, Americans emphasize individualism, while Japanese put stress on groups, such as family and workplace. Also, Americans tend to have looser and
5　more tentative relationships with others than Japanese who have more solid and lasting ties. In addition, Americans favor assertiveness. In contrast, Japanese favor understatements. Moreover, unlike Americans who believe in the power of words, Japanese stress the importance of silence. Finally, Americans value rational understanding, but it is intuition that is emphasized among Japanese. In these ways, Dr.
10　Barnlund pointed out several differences in communicative styles between Americans and Japanese. However, this represents a rather stereotypical view of cultural differences prominent in the 80s, and today we cannot categorize the two groups so clearly as he did.

Basis of contrast \ People	Americans	Japanese
① emphasize . . . ② have . . . ③ favor . . . ④ believe in . . . ⑤ value . . .	individualism assertiveness	more solid and lasting ties

Rhetoric 3 — Contrastの文章とは

Comparisonの文章は2つのものごとの類似点を述べるものだったが、contrastは相違点を述べるものである。Contrastの文章を書く場合も、comparison同様、次の2点に注意する必要がある。

1) **同じ種類**のものごとを対比する。
　　例： ○ 男性 vs. 女性　　× 男性 vs. 子供
2) **同一の基準**でものごとを対比する。
　　例： ○ A大学の学生数 vs. B大学の学生数
　　　　× A大学の学生数 vs. B大学の女子学生数

Model 2 では、1) アメリカ人と日本人という2つの異なる「国民」を、2)「他人とのコミュニケーションの仕方」という「同一の基準」で対比している。

Rhetoric 4 — Contrastの文章にまつわる表現

Contrastの文章を書く上で大切な表現を学習しよう。Model 2 で用いられていた表現は波線で示してあるので確認しよう。

1) 文と文を結びつけるもの： however, on the other hand, in contrast

- Americans favor assertiveness. $\begin{Bmatrix} \text{In contrast,} \\ \text{On the other hand,} \\ \text{However,} \end{Bmatrix}$ Japanese favor understatements.

2) 節と節を結びつけるもの： while, whereas, but, yet, although, though

- Americans emphasize individualism, $\begin{Bmatrix} \text{while} \\ \text{whereas} \end{Bmatrix}$ Japanese put stress on groups, such as family and workplace.

- Americans value rational understanding, $\begin{Bmatrix} \text{but} \\ \text{yet} \end{Bmatrix}$ it is intuition that is emphasized among Japanese.

3) その他: unlike, different from
- $\left\{\begin{array}{l}\text{Unlike}\\ \text{Different from}\end{array}\right\}$ Americans who believe in the power of words, Japanese stress the importance of silence.

4) 比較級
- Americans try to have looser and more tentative relationships with others than Japanese who have more solid and lasting ties.

5) 反対語
- loose   vs. solid
- tentative   vs. lasting
- assertiveness   vs. understatements
- rational understanding vs. intuition

Exercise 2

次の表はサッカーと野球を対比し、両者の5つの相違点をまとめたものです。おのおのの相違点を与えられた語句を使って表現しなさい。

Basis of contrast / Sport	Soccer	Baseball
① origin	Great Britain	America
② number of players	11	9
③ major equipment	ball	ball, glove, bat
④ playing time	fixed	not fixed
⑤ history as a professional sport in Japan	short	long

① (on the other hand) Soccer originated in ...

② (whereas) Eleven members are necessary for a soccer team, ...

③ (Unlike) Unlike soccer which uses only a ball, ...

④ (but) The playing time for a soccer game is ...

⑤ (反対語、比較級 [shorter / longer]、than) Professional soccer in Japan has a ...

Exercise 3

Exercise 2で書いた①〜⑤の各文を paragraph の形にまとめなさい。

3. Comparison and Contrast (類似点と相違点)

Task 3

次の文章を読み、アウトラインを完成しなさい。完全な形にまとめる必要はありません。メモの形でかまいません。

Model 3

Yakiniku and *Bulgogi*

Korea and Japan are neighboring countries. They share many cultural similarities. One such aspect may be their eating habits. Although these things might have emerged from similar habits, the two countries have developed their distinct characteristics over time. One such example may be the way in which beef is grilled. Grilled beef is called *yakiniku* in Japanese, and in Korean it is called *bulgogi*. There are many similarities and differences between Japanese *yakiniku* and Korean *bulgogi*.

One similarity, which is easy to spot, is where one cooks the grilled beef. Both *yakiniku* and *bulgogi* are cooked right at the table, not in the kitchen like most dishes, regardless of whether they are cooked at home or at a restaurant. Grilling at a table is a lot of fun and meat tastes much better when it is eaten promptly after it is cooked. Another similarity is that when Korean people eat *bulgogi*, they usually eat with friends and family. Likewise, Japanese almost always have *yakiniku* in a group or with their family or companions, too.

On the other hand, there are some differences, too. First of all, the beef parts of the cow eaten are different. Japanese people eat not only the lean meat, but they also eat the internal organs, such as liver, intestines, and heart. In contrast, Korean people eat only the lean meat. Another difference can be observed in how the uncooked meat is served at the table. In Japan, bite-sized pieces of meat are served on a plate when we cook *yakiniku*. However, in Korea, blocks of meat are placed on the table. These blocks of meat are grilled and then cut into small pieces with scissors before being eaten. In other words, scissors are always one of the utensils on the table when eating *bulgogi*. Moreover, how people eat *yakiniku* and *bulgogi* are different. When Japanese eat *yakiniku*, the meat and vegetables are dipped into a sauce. However, with *bulgogi*, the meat is never dipped into a sauce. Instead, the meat is marinated in the sauce before cooking. In addition to the sauce, *kimchi* and garlic are used as a flavoring. The mixture is then placed on a lettuce leaf or other green leafy vegetables, rolled and eaten.

We can observe the similarities and differences in the way Japanese and Koreans grill beef. The similarities enable us to experience an enjoyable atmosphere with friends at the table, and the differences enable us to enjoy the different taste of delicious meat. In sum, that is why both *yakiniku* and *bulgogi* are highly valued as not only being delicious but also memorable dishes.

OUTLINE

Yakiniku and *Bulgogi*

I. There are many similarities and [1]_____ between Japanese [2]_____ and Korean [3]_____.
II. Similarities
   A. Cooked right at the table
   B. Eaten with friends and family
III. [4]_____
   A. Which beef parts of cow are eaten
     1. *Yakiniku*: lean meat and [5]_____
     2. *Bulgogi*: only [6]_____
   B. How the uncooked meat is served
     1. *Yakiniku*: [7]_____ of meat served on a plate
     2. *Bulgogi*: [8]_____ of meat served on the table and cut with [9]_____
   C. How the meat is eaten
     1. *Yakiniku*: dipped into a [10]_____
     2. *Bulgogi*: [11]_____ before cooking, flavored with [12]_____ [13]_____ on a lettuce leaf or other leafy vegetables
IV. We can observe similarities and differences in [14]_____. The similarities enable us to experience [15]_____, while the [16]_____ enable us to enjoy [17]_____.

Rhetoric 5 — Comparison and Contrast とは

Comparison と contrast をまとめた文章が comparison and contrast である。つまり comparison and contrast とは、2つのものごとの類似点と相違点を両方説明したものである。通常いくつかの類似点をまず述べ、次いで相違点をいくつか述べていく方法で書かれる。

Exercise 4

Model 3 において、Rhetoric 2 と 4 で学んだ表現がどのように使われているか確認しなさい。また、Rhetoric 2 と 4 で扱わなかった表現も確認しなさい。

On Your Own

(1) Model 2 では日本人とアメリカ人の相違点が示されていたが、両者の類似点としてはどのようなものがあるか考え、説明しなさい。

(2) 5年前のあなたと現在のあなたを比べ、変わらない面と違っている面をいくつかあげ、説明しなさい。

(3) 下記の表1に示されているピザとお好み焼きの相似点と相違点を説明する essay を書きなさい。

	Pizza	*Okonomiyaki*
Similarities		
1. Who we eat it with …	Eat with companions	Eat with companions
2. What parts it has …	A crust and toppings	A crust and toppings
3. How it is eaten …	Cut into pieces	Cut into pieces
Differences		
1. Where it comes from …	Italy	Japan
2. What it is made of …	A lot of cheese and tomatoes	No cheese or tomatoes
3. What it is made of …	No cabbage or seaweed	A lot of cabbage and seaweed

表1　ピザとお好み焼きの類似点と相違点

Chapter 11　Cause and Effect
事象の原因と結果について論理的に書いてみよう

Cause and effect（原因と結果）を説明する文章においては、cause と effect との間の因果関係を整理して論理的に説明することが求められている。

1. 原因に重点を置く文 (Focus on Cause)

Task 1

次の例文は最近の少子問題についてその原因をいくつか述べている。この文章を読んで、何が結果であり、何がその原因としてあげられているか、整理しよう。

Why Aren't There More Children?　🔊 13

　　Recently, the birthrate in Japan has been declining dramatically. Why do married women hesitate to have babies? It is not that married women do not want to have children, but rather they are afraid that bringing up children is quite difficult in Japan, especially in Tokyo. There are many reasons to explain why Japanese women may
5　be reluctant to have large families.

　　First, owing to the high cost of living, many young couples are forced to live in small houses or apartments; therefore, it is not easy to share this small space with many children. In addition, moving to a bigger place is not an easy option.

　　Second, as Japan is an academic credential society, many children go to cram
10　schools besides ordinary schools, so parents have to pay a large sum of money for education. Consequently, young couples feel the need to have fewer children because of the high cost of education.

　　Moreover, in the past decades, Japanese women's sense of values have changed. Marriage and having children were once thought to be the only happiness for wom-
15　en, but women who have higher levels of education now think there are other goals to live by beside child-rearing.

　　Even if some women decide to have children and a career, they worry whether they can continue working while taking care of their children. That is because there is not enough public support available for working parents, such as public daycare
20　facilities or child-leave.

Hence, the decline of the birthrate is not due to the selfishness of young couples, but can be attributed to insufficient public support systems among other things. Maybe providing sufficient public facilities to support young working mothers will be the first step in order to prevent the decline of the birthrate.

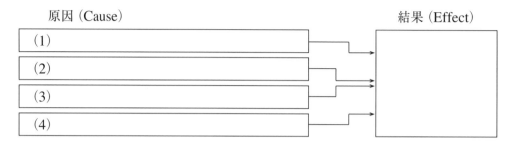

Task 1 で書かれているものはある事象（結果）に対する原因が詳しく述べられているもので、このような文を「原因に重点を置く文」(Focus on cause) という。これとは逆に「結果に重点を置く文」(Focus on effect) もある。

2. 結果に重点を置く文 (Focus on Effect)

Task 2

次の文を読んで表を完成しよう。

An Uncomfortable Place to Live 　🔊 14

　　Tokyo is not a very comfortable place to live in. Everything, ranging from people to office buildings, is centralized in this city. As a result, Tokyo has become too crowded. Because of this centralization, people living in this city have to face some uncomfortable situations.

5　　First, most of the streets and roads are full of cars and other vehicles. Thus, there are always traffic jams here and there.

　　Second, the prices of commodities are higher than most cities in the world. Land prices are outrageously high. Because of this, people who live in the suburbs are forced to commute long distances to their offices. They have to put up with not 10 only long hours of commuting but also very crowded trains. By the time they reach their offices, they are already exhausted.

　　Third, the concentration of people and cars has made the environment worse. Rivers are polluted with drainage and the taste of drinking water is poor. The air is also polluted, causing environmentally-related diseases, such as lung cancer and allergies.

15　　　Due to the fact that there are many people and cars, the streets are full of noise. It is very hard to find a moment of silence in Tokyo.

　　　In conclusion, the quality of life in Tokyo is very poor. It is a big question why so many people want to live in this stifling city.

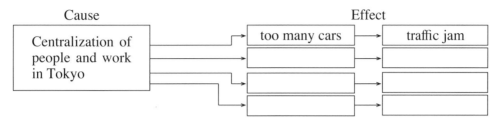

Rhetoric 1 —— 原因と結果を表す表現

原因と結果を表す表現には次のようなものがある（句読点の使い方にも注意する）。

(1) {節/文} (cause) と {節/文} (effect) を結び付けるもの：

I got lost; {as a result, / consequently, / therefore, / because of this,} I was late for the meeting.

I lost my purse. {As a result, / Consequently, / Therefore, / Because of this,} I could not do the shopping.

(2) 節 (cause) と節 (effect) を結び付けるもの：

{Since / Because / Due to the fact (that)} I did not get up early, I was late for school.

(3) その他

結果が主語になっているもの：

Liver cancer may {result from / be due to / follow from} too much drinking.

原因が主語になっているもの：

Too much drinking may {result in / cause / be responsible for / lead to} liver cancer.

Exercise 1

次の原因と結果を表している文章を、いろいろな表現を使って書いてみよう。

1. I had exceeded the speed limit. I was charged a fine.
   - （1） because を使って：
   - （2） as a result を使って：
   - （3） therefore を使って：
2. Too much smoking can cause lung cancer.
   - （1） result in を使って：
   - （2） result from を使って：
3. I almost drowned when I was a small child. I am still afraid of water.
   - （1） My fear of water で始まる文に：
   - （2） My experience of near drowning で始まる文に：

Rhetoric 2 — 条件・仮定を表す表現

Many young couples live in small apartments; therefore, they cannot have many children.
この文を if を使って書き直すと次のようになる。

If they lived in larger apartments, they could have many children.
このように、現実にないことを想定して述べる文を仮定法という。

仮定法にはいろいろな種類があるが、ここではもっともよく使われる「仮定法過去」と「仮定法過去完了」について整理しておこう。

- 仮定法過去：「現在の事実に反する仮定」を表す。

  If ...（過去形），... 過去形助動詞 + 原形動詞 ...

  （もし（今）...なら、（今）...だろうに。）

  If I had a lot of money, I would buy a large house.

- 仮定法過去完了：「過去の事実に反する仮定」を表す。

  If ... had + 過去分詞 ... ，... 過去形助動詞 + have + 過去分詞 ...

  （もし（あの時）...していたら、（あの時）...であったろうに。）

  If I had had a lot of money, I would have bought a large house.

- **if-clause**(節) が省略されているもの：

  To hear her speak English（＝If you hear her speak English）, you would take her for an American.

  （彼女が英語を話すのを聞いたら、あなたは彼女がアメリカ人と間違えるであろう。）

  With your help（＝If I had your help）, I should succeed.

  （あなたの助けがあれば、成功するのだが。）

  But for your help（＝If he had not had your help）, he would not have been so successful.

  （あなたの助けがなかったら、彼はあれほど成功しなかったであろう。）

- **I wish に続く仮定法**：

    I wish I were a bird and could fly freely in the sky.

    （わたしが鳥で、自由に空が飛べたらなあ。）

    I wish I had studied harder for the examination.

    （試験勉強をもっとしておいたらよかったなあ。）

Exercise 2
次の文の誤りを直しなさい。
1. I wish I can go abroad to study.

2. If I had left home by 8:00 this morning, I will arrive at Kyoto by noon.

3. You might have passed the entrance examination if you studied harder.

Exercise 3
次の文章を事実に反する文、つまり仮定法を使った文に書き変えなさい。
1. This university does not have good facilities. Therefore, it does not have many applicants.

2. We did not oppose the construction of the dam five years ago. As a result, the nature around the dam has been damaged a great deal.

3. We allowed the government to increase the sales tax. Consequently, we are now suffering from the high cost of living.

4. As I did not have enough money, I did not pay you back at that time.

On Your Own
次のトピックで原因と結果を表す文章を書きなさい。
(1) 食べ過ぎ (overeating) がもたらす結果について考え、結果に重点を置く文章を書きなさい。
(2) 円高がもたらす日本の経済への影響について、結果に重点を置く文章を書きなさい。（自分の身近なところで観察できる範囲内で）
(3) 好きな課目と成績との関係について、重点を原因あるいは結果どちらかにおいて文章を書きなさい。

Vocabulary (1) ── アカデミックな文体にするために

文全体のスタイルとしても論文にあったスタイルというものがある。それらの多くは簡単な約束事である。これらをマスターすることだけで、文章の格調が格段に高まる。

① 縮約形を使わない

We don't know the result until the experiment is concluded.

→ We do not know the result until the experiment is concluded.

There haven't been any major solutions that were implemented.

→ There have not been any major solutions that were implemented.

② 硬い否定表現を使う
- Not ... any → no

  We have not obtained any information on that matter.

  → We have obtained no information on that matter.
- Not ... much → little

  It does not appear to have much effect on performance.

  → It appears to have little effect on performance.
- Not ... many → few

  Many countries do not have appropriate regulations, or do not enforce them.

  → Few countries have appropriate regulations, or do not enforce them.

③ 直接疑問文の使用を少なくする

What can we draw from this result?

→ We need to consider what we can draw from this result.

④ 代名詞 you の使用を避ける

You can see the result in Table 1.

→ The result is shown in Table 1.

⑤ 副詞・文副詞を文頭や文末でなく、動詞のそばの文中に入れ込む。
これだけで文の格調が高まる。

The symptom was diagnosed carefully.

→ The symptom was carefully diagnosed.

However, it is not difficult to do such kind of experiment.

→ It is, however, not difficult to do such kind of experiment.

Exercise 4

次の文をよりアカデミックな文体に変えなさい。

1. An increasing number of infectious diseases has been reported from neighboring countries recently.
2. While the aid is reaching many locations now, access to safe drinking water remains inadequate.
3. What can we do to tackle the environmental risks to our children?
4. Drug development is expensive and time consuming and doesn't always lead to a marketable product.
5. This clearly wouldn't have been possible without the strong commitment of the group.
6. You can check the statistical data in ten tables and four graphs.

Vocabulary (2) — Mnemonics (記憶術)

"Mnemonics" と呼ばれる「語呂合わせ」などの記憶術は、音と対応しない綴字や規則的なパターンに従わない例外的な綴字を覚える際に活用されている。下記の1〜5は mnemonics の例である (Edward Fry, 1992)。よく読んで、それぞれの関係をつかんでおこう。

1. **Little Words in Big Words:** ある語の中に別の語が含まれ、両者の間には微かな意味のつながりがある場合もある。
   例： principal — pal　　hear — ear　　naturally — rally
   　　 cordial — dial　　instead — tea　　miscellaneous — cell
2. **Sentence of Exception Words:** 同一の綴字部分が異なって発音される語をひとまとめにして文を作り、綴字と発音を確認する。
   例： "ough" の綴字を持つ語：I thought I bought enough cough syrup to make it through this rough tough winter.
   　　 "ei" の綴字を持つ語：Neither foreigner had a weird height either.
3. **Letter Visualizations:** 意味を視覚を使って確認する。
   例： You need both "i's" for skiing.
   　　 The last letter is curved in arc (not in ark).
4. **Acronyms:** 最初の文字を組み合わせた略語として覚える。
   例： arithmetic — A Rat In The House Might Eat The Ice Cream
5. **Clever Links:** 類似した単語を使って、しゃれた文を作る。
   例： A shepherd herds sheep.
   　　 Miss Pell can't spell. (double "s" for "misspell")
   　　 There is no X (rating) for ecstasy.
   　　 There is a rat in separate.
   　　 You hammer a stake, but eat a steak.

Chapter 12   Argumentation
論理的で説得力のある論証文を書こう

　Argumentation の目的は、自分（書き手）と異なる意見を持つ人に対し、自分の意見の正しさを示し、自分の意見を受け入れるよう説得することが目的である。そのためには、**論理的で、説得力のある文**を書かなくてはいけない。そのための方策を探ってみよう。

Task 1

　次の2つの文章は、いずれも "The government should build more bike-only lanes." という主張をするために書かれたものである。それぞれを読んでどちらの方が説得力があるか、そしてそれはなぜか考えてみよう。

(A)   More Bike-only Lanes

　(1) Although we know that riding bicycles is good for our health and that using bicycles saves money and energy, there is one problem in present-day Japan that prevents the promotion of cycling. (2) That is, there are some places with bike-only lanes in Japan, but the number of those lanes is not enough for riders to enjoy cycling safely and comfortably. (3) Therefore, the government should build more bike-only lanes in order to promote more cycling.

　(4) First of all, under the present conditions, cycling is very dangerous not only for bike users but also for people around them. (5) According to a survey from the Ministry of Internal Affairs and Communications (2011), the number of accidents involving cyclists is increasing. (6) Some cyclists choose to ride on sidewalks among pedestrians, which is actually an infringement of the law. (7) In addition, we often see bicycle riders among traffic with speeding cars, too. (8) As a result, they crash into pedestrians, or they are hit by cars, resulting in heavy casualties.

　(9) Secondly, if people know that they can bike safely using the bike-only lanes, more people will opt for bicycles instead of cars. (10) They would not want to use bikes unless they feel they are safe on the roads. (11) This would in turn decrease the number of cars on the road.

　(12) Thirdly, other countries have already proved that there are several benefits of building bike-only lanes. (13) The Netherlands and Germany built extensive bike-only lanes, claiming that promoting bicycling is the best way to solve several problems: carbon dioxide emission, traffic jams, and lack of exercise. (14) In 1999 the U.S. Con-

gress also passed a bill that promoted the construction of bike-only ways.

(15) Although there are problems associated with building bike-only lanes, once they are built, they offer us many benefits. (16) Therefore, the Japanese government should consider building bike-only lanes as a national policy.

(B) More Bike Lanes

(1) I like riding a bicycle. (2) I often use my bicycle when I go out. (3) I think everyone would be happy if the government builds bike-only lanes all over Japan. (4) The last time I went out shopping by bicycle, there was no sidewalk on the way, and I had to ride on roads where there were also a lot of cars. (5) Many cars passed close by me at high speed. (6) I was very afraid of them crashing into me. (7) But it is sometimes fun to ride on the roads because passing cars on the narrow road is exciting.

(8) And if there were bike-only lanes, pedestrians would feel happy, too. (9) My grandmother likes taking a walk when the weather is beautiful. (10) She often complains about the bicycles riding on sidewalks. (11) But for cyclists, riding on the sidewalks is safer than riding on the roads, so I cannot say clearly which is better, riding on the road or riding on the sidewalks.

(12) Building bike-only lanes is a good idea, but I think it is difficult to implement this idea. (13) Japan is a small country with little space to build bike-only lanes. (14) And we need a lot of money to build these lanes. (15) I don't want to pay a large amount of tax. (16) So in order to make bike-only lanes, the government should first consider how to cut other expenditures.

Task 2

（A）と（B）の文に関し、次の手順で分析を行ってみよう。
（1）まず、それぞれの文章の中で、書き手の主張がもっともよく出ている文 (thesis statement) を見つけ出し、（T）のマークをつける。
（2）それぞれの一文ごとに、自転車専用レーン建設を勧める立場に立った見解に対しては **For** を、自転車専用レーン建設の弊害を述べている文には **Against** をつけなさい。また、どちらとも取れないものには **Neutral** とつけなさい。

	(A)		(B)
(1)	For	(1)	Neutral
(2)		(2)	
(3)		(3)	
(4)		(4)	
(5)		(5)	

（6）　　　　　　　（6）
（7）　　　　　　　（7）
（8）　　　　　　　（8）
（9）　　　　　　　（9）
（10）　　　　　　（10）
（11）　　　　　　（11）
（12）　　　　　　（12）
（13）　　　　　　（13）
（14）　　　　　　（14）
（15）　　　　　　（15）
（16）　　　　　　（16）

Task 3

Task 2 で行った分析結果から（A）と（B）の違いについてどのようなことが言えますか。

Rhetoric 1 ― Inner-argumentation analysis

Task 2 でしたような分析を inner-argumentation analysis と呼ぶ。

（A）と（B）の argumentative pattern（論点の推移のパターン）は次のようになる。（右肩についている数字は、論点が変更された回数を示す）

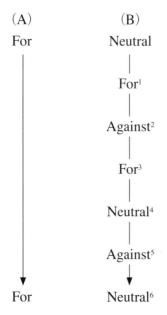

この図を見ると、（A）と（B）の論点の推移がよくわかる。（A）の場合は、最初に書き手が持った論点が最後まで変わらず貫かれている。それに対し、（B）は論点がさまざまに変わり、しかも thesis statement がはっきりと提出されてない。論点はどっちつかずの

Neutral で始まり、文章の最後も Neutral で終わり、結局「bike-only lane を建設すべき」という主張があやふやな形で終わっている。

これが、Chapter 6 (p. 36) で紹介された英語に代表される「**直線的な論理展開**」(上記 (A) で表されたもの) と日本語によく見られる「**渦巻き型の論理展開**」((B) に見られるようなもの) の証明とも言える。

Exercise 1

Task 1 の (A) の文章のアウトラインを完成させなさい。

Argument: The government should build bike-only lanes.

 I. (第 1 の理由): _____
 II. (第 2 の理由): _____
 III. (第 3 の理由): _____

Rhetoric 2 ── より堅固な argumentative essay 構築のために

論証文 (argumentative essay) では自分の主張をぐらつかせず、一直線に述べることの大切さが理解できたと思う。ここで、より堅固な論証文 (argumentative essay) を構築するために、もう一段階踏み込むことの重要性を述べたい。それは、自分の論を主張するだけでなく、自分とは反対の意見を持つ人からの予想される反対意見を提示し、それに対してなぜその考えに自分は同意できないかを述べることにより、自分の意見の優位性の論証を試みるものである。(B) には不十分ながらそのような見解は示されている。ただ、その示し方が、ただ単に述べられてあるというだけであり、構成 (organization) としては inner-argumentation analysis で見たとおり、論旨があっちへ行ったりこっちへ行ったりしているものであり、読み手にその主張はストレートには伝わってこない。

しっかりとした論証文の基本的アウトラインは、次のようなものになる。

 I. 主題文 (thesis statement) ＝問題に関し、自分のとる立場を明確にする。
 II. 自分の意見をサポートする第 1 の理由
  1. 詳しい説明・具体例
  2. 詳しい説明・具体例
 III. 自分の意見をサポートする第 2 の理由
  1. 詳しい説明・具体例
  2. 詳しい説明・具体例
 IV. 自分の意見をサポートする第 3 の理由
  1. 詳しい説明・具体例
  2. 詳しい説明・具体例
 V. 自分の意見と反対の意見＋それに対する反論
 VI. 結論＝今までの意見をまとめ、自分の主張をもう一度強調する。

上記のアウトラインに基づいて (A) の文章を書き直したものが次のものである。

More Bike-only Lanes

🔊 17

Although we know that riding bicycles is good for our health and that using bicycles saves money and energy, there is one problem in present-day Japan that prevents the promotion of cycling. That is, there are some places with bike-only lanes in Japan but the number of those lanes is not enough for riders to enjoy cycling safely and comfortably. Therefore, the government should build more bike-only lanes in order to promote more cycling.

First of all, under the present conditions, cycling is very dangerous not only for bike users but also for people around them. According to a survey from the Ministry of Internal Affairs and Communications, the number of accidents involving cyclists is increasing. Some cyclists choose to ride on sidewalks among pedestrians, which is actually an infringement of the law. In addition, we often see bicycle riders among speeding cars, too. As a result, they crash into pedestrians, or they are hit by cars, resulting in heavy casualties.

Secondly, if people know that they can bike safely using the bike-only lanes, more people will opt for bicycles instead of cars. They would not want to use bikes unless they feel they are safe on the roads. This would in turn decrease the number of cars on the road.

Thirdly, other countries have already proved that there are several benefits of building bike-only lanes. The Netherlands and Germany built extensive bike-only lanes, claiming that promoting bicycles is the best way to solve several problems: carbon dioxide emission, traffic jams, and lack of exercise. In 1999 the U.S. Congress also passed a bill that promoted the construction of bike-only ways.

It is true that we need to solve some problems in order to build bike-only lanes all over Japan. The biggest problem with building such lanes in Japan is that we do not have extra space on the roads, and it may cost a lot if we try to widen the roads further. However, this problem will be overcome if we seriously consider our safety, environment, and health.

Although there are problems associated with building bike-only lanes, once they are built, they offer us many benefits. Therefore, the Japanese government should consider building bike-only lanes as a national policy.

第5パラグラフ目に付け加わったものは、「予想される反対意見への反論」として、「自転車専用レーン建設の難しさについては十分承知しているが、それを考慮しても、建設の方がメリットが大きいのだ」ということをさらに強調して述べている。筆者はさまざまなことを考慮したうえで自説を主張しているのだ、という態度を示すことにより、論証も盤石なものとなる。

Rhetoric 3 ── 説得力のある argumentative essay を書くために

Argumentative essay というのは、ある事例に対し自分の意見を持ち、読み手に自分の

意見の正しさを納得させ、自分の意見を受け入れさせることを目的としている。Argumentative essay というのは、たいていの場合、ある問題（往々にして相反する意見が並立する問題）に対し、書き手はどちらかの考えを持ち、その考えの正当さを力強く説き、読み手を説得しなければならない。

Argumentative essay を書くうえで重要なポイント：
(1) audience（読み手）の存在を強く意識する。
(2) 書く前に自分の意見をはっきりと持つ。
(3) 読み手はあなたの意見と相反する考えを持っていると仮定する。
(4) 自分の考えを書いている途中でぐらつかせない。
(5) あくまでも問題に関し議論することが重要であり、自分と異なる意見を持つ人の人格攻撃となるような書き方は慎む。

つまり、客観的に、論理的に一貫した論を進めることが重要である。

Rhetoric 4 ── 客観的で論理的な文章を書くために

自分の主張する論点の正当さを読み手に納得させるために、具体的には次の要点を論拠として取り込んだ文章にするといい。
(1) 事実を挙げたり、統計的数字を出す。
(2) 例をいくつか示す。
(3) 権威者からの引用をする。

こうした、いわば自分の主張の証拠と言えるものを十分に文章の中に取り入れることにより、相手に反論の余地を与えず、自分の主張を貫くことができる。

そこで、その論の進め方として大きく分けて2通りの方法がある。
Inductive reasoning と deductive reasoning である。

Inductive reasoning というのは個々の特殊な例の積み重ねから一般原則に導くものである。それに対し、**deductive reasoning** というのは、まず最初に一般原則を述べてしまい、あとからその主張のサポートとなる理由や個々の事例をあげていくものである。

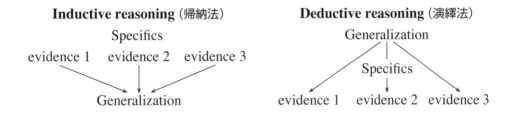

自分の主張を相手に説得する場合、inductive reasoning をとるか、あるいは deductive reasoning にするかは、事例や読み手の性格を考えてどちらが効果的かを考えて判断する。日本語の場合はどちらかと言うと、inductive reasoning で展開されることを好むが、**英語の文章、ことに argumentative essay では自分の主張を冒頭で述べる deductive reasoning**

の方が一般的であり、より効果的である。

Exercise 2

次の文章に関し、これまでに学んだことをもとにして各問いに答えなさい。
（1） 次の文章は inductive reasoning（帰納法）で書かれていますか、それとも deductive reasoning（演繹法）で書かれていますか。
（2） 次の文章を5つの paragraph に分けるとすると、どのようになりますか。paragraph の切れ目の箇所を P で示しなさい。
（3） この文章全体の thesis statement を探し出し、下線を引きなさい。
（4） この文章でどの部分が Rhetoric 3 と Rhetoric 4 で述べられているポイントに従って書かれているか答えなさい。

Dangers of Smoking

Today there are still some smokers who enjoy smoking while ignoring the unwholesome effects of their habit. Smokers should realize the negative effects of smoking — not only to themselves, but to those with whom they have contact. It is common knowledge that smokers develop lung cancer at much higher rates than nonsmokers. The rate of contracting cancer of the larynx is twenty times higher in smokers as compared to nonsmokers, while that of lung cancer is four times higher (*Global Health Survey*, 2010). Adverse effects are not only inflicted upon the smokers themselves. The smoke is extremely harmful to those people who are in close proximity to the smokers. Tobacco smoke is usually classified into two main types: primary smoke and secondary smoke. Primary smoke is that which the smokers inhale themselves; secondary smoke is the smoke that emanates from the lit cigarette that is passively inhaled by the people in the smokers' close environment. Dr. White, a famous *cardiovascular specialist, says that secondary smoke actually has the potential for being more harmful than primary smoke. This is because secondary smoke contains 2.8 times more nicotine, 3.4 times more tar and 4.7 times more carbon monoxide than the primary smoke. Those who are in close proximity to the smokers inhale both the primary smoke and the secondary smoke. Thus, nonsmokers are often poisoned by smokers against their own will. The harmful effects of smoking are not only limited to those who are exposed at that specific moment. Smoking also has a long-term effect on subsequent generations. According to a report published by the Cancer Association in 2008, the rate of premature births among nonsmoking mothers is 2.8%, while that among smoking mothers is 9.2%. In conclusion, considering these facts, smokers should realize what harm smoking does to those around them as well as their own bodies.

（*循環器の専門医）

Rhetoric 5 — 「すべきである」という表現

Argumentative essay の場合よく出てくる表現として、「すべきである」というのがある。この意味のいろいろな表現とその語法を見てみよう。

(1) 動詞＋**that**＋動詞の原形

（主節の動詞の時制に関係なく原形を取る。should を前に取ることもある）

I recommend that Mary (should) go to her parents' home immediately.

My teacher insisted that I attend the meeting in London.

It has been suggested that the government be responsible for the action.

このパターンを取るほかの動詞：

advise, ask, beg, demand, desire, insist, propose, request, require など

(2) 動詞＋目的語＋不定詞

I strongly urge you to go to the doctor immediately.

They asked him to consider his responsibility once again.

このパターンを取るほかの動詞：

advise, ask, beg, desire, forbid, request, require など

(3) 形容詞を用いて

It is advisable that she (should) leave here before the rush-hour traffic begins.

It is urgent that he get my message as soon as possible.

このパターンを取るほかの形容詞：

crucial, essential, desirable, good (better, best), important, necessary など

Exercise 3

（　）の中の単語を使って 10 語以上の短文を書きなさい。

1. （demand） _____
2. （insist） _____
3. （essential） _____

On Your Own

次のそれぞれの対立する議論に関し、どちらかの立場を取り、それを主張する argumentative essay を書きなさい。

(1) In order to learn a foreign language, it is essential / not essential to go to the country where the language is spoken and live there for a while.

(2) Do you think it is better to live in an urban city? Or do you think it is better to live in a rural town?

(3) Ordinary citizens should / should not be allowed to carry handguns.

(4) Toy commercials should / should not be aired during children's programs.

Chapter 13　Letter Writing

英文の手紙の書き方を学ぼう

学生である皆さんが一番書く機会が多いと思われるのは外国の企業や大学への **a letter of application**（応募の手紙）かも知れない。それを中心に英語の手紙文の書き方を学ぼう。

Task 1
ある日、大学の掲示板に次のような掲示があった。

ABC College in the U.S.A. will offer a scholarship of one year study for a Japanese student. Anybody interested should contact Mr. Thompson of ABC College at the following address:

　　Mr. Thompson
　　Office of Admissions, ABC College

次のサンプル (A), (B) はこの掲示にもとづいて書かれたものである。この両者を比べて内容や手紙の調子にどのような違いがあるか考えてみよう

──────── (A) ────────

Dear Mr. Thompson:

　　My name is Hisayo Takada. I am twenty years old and I go to Toyo Academy. I am interested in American people and culture. But I have never been to a foreign country. I want to go to America very much.

　　Of course, I am studying very hard everyday.

　　My brother is still a high school student and my parents just recently built a new house. Going to America costs a lot of money. So I need the scholarship.

　　If I can go to ABC College I will study harder than now and I want to make many foreign friends there. I think American people are very friendly and kind. Surely I will have a nice relationship with them.

　　Mr. Thompson, I want to know American people and culture. Please give me the chance. After a year, I will grow more than now.

　　I wait for your answer.

　　　　　　　　　　　　　　　　　　　　　　　　Takada

(B)

Dear Mr. Thompson:

 I would like to apply for admission to ABC College, specifically for entrance into the Business Administration program. I hope to pursue a career in international business in the future.

 I am presently a high school senior at Menno West High School in West Bend, Colorado. I have a 3.8 grade point average on a 4.0 scale. In addition, my SAT score is in the upper 20% bracket.

 For the last five years, I have been helping my father in his commercial building maintenance business, including extensive bookkeeping and sales work. I believe that I have the academic credentials and work experience to do well in your business program.

 I am interested in applying for your scholarship. Would you kindly send an application form to me at the above address?

 Thank you very much.

Sincerely yours,
David Anderson

内容：
(A) に書かれている事実
 1. _____
 2. _____
(B) に書かれている事実
 1. _____
 2. _____

調子：
(A) の手紙の調子 _____

(B) の手紙の調子 _____

Rhetoric 1 —— 応募の手紙と礼状

 英語で書く応募の手紙では**客観的な事実**を中心に書く必要がある。また、手紙の調子も**自分が応募する人間にふさわしいという自信に満ちた**ものでなくてはならない。(A) のサンプルのような日本人にありがちの**情に訴える**という手紙の調子では同情されるどころか、弱い人間と見なされ、受け入れられない公算が大きい。

Task 2

次に就職のための応募の手紙文（a letter of application to a company）のサンプルを検討し、以下の課題について考えてみよう。

28-29, Yayoi-cho
Nerima-ku, Tokyo 176–0000
December 15, 2024

Mr. James Brown
President
ABC Associates
123 Otemachi
Chiyoda-ku, Tokyo 100-0004

Dear Mr. Brown: 🔊 21

 I am writing in response to your advertisement in *The Japan Daily* on December 1.
 Having worked in the field of domestic sales for nearly six years, I am very interested in the challenges of international sales. I have followed your parent company with interest for some time. I greatly admire it for its extraordinary growth and profitability.
 Experienced in both inside and outside sales, I believe that I am qualified for the position of sales manager. As documented in my accompanying resume, I also have three years of experience in management and was twice selected as "Product Manager of the Year."
 I look forward to meeting with ABC Association to further discuss this exciting and challenging opportunity.

Sincerely yours,

Michiko Suzuki
Michiko Suzuki

就職の応募の手紙の場合は、次のような要件が必要である。それぞれはこの手紙のどの文に相当するであろうか。当てはまる文を見つけだし、線を引いてそれぞれの番号を付けよう。

(1) 読み手にどのようにして応募のことを知ったかを伝える。
(2) 読み手になぜその会社に興味を持ったかを伝える。
(3) 読み手に自分がその仕事にふさわしいということを示す。

(4) 募集している側では何十、何百という応募の手紙を見ていることであろう。その中で自分のものが注目に価するということを示す。
(5) 面接の機会を求めているということを示す。

Exercise 1

A letter of application とともによく書く機会があるのはお礼状 (a thank-you note) である。次の例を参考にしてホームステイ先への礼状を書いてみよう。

Dear Mr. And Mrs. Jones, 　　　　　　　　　　　　　🔊 22

　　I would like to thank you again for the wonderful stay I had with you last summer. It has been three weeks since I came home, but I just cannot forget the exciting time I had in the U.S. In particular, the stay with you has given me a lasting impression. I loved every moment at your place. Our tour to Lake Washington was the highlight for me. I have never had such a wonderful time.

　　I am back at school now. I seem to understand everything my teacher says in my English class better than before. I am sure that my English has greatly improved.

　　　　　　　　　　　　　　　　　　　　　　Sincerely yours,

　　　　　　　　　　　　　　　　　　　　　Tsutomu Yamaguchi

　　　　　　　　　　　　　　　　　　　　　Tsutomu Yamaguchi

Rhetoric 2 — Letter Writing の基礎知識

(1) 封筒の書き方

Tsutomu Yamaguchi
1-2, Midori-cho 3-chome
Koganei-shi, Tokyo
184-0003 　JAPAN

　　　　　　　　Mr. and Mrs. Thomas Jones
　　　　　　　　321 Lakeside Lane
　　　　　　　　Mankato, MN　56001
　　　　　　　　U.S.A.

[切手]

---

(2) 住所によく使われる略号

Apt. = Apartment	Fl. = Floor	c/o = in care of
Co. = Company	Ltd. = Limited	Inc. = Incorporated
No. = Number	P.O. = Post Office	Ave. = Avenue

Blvd. = Boulevard　　　Dr. = Drive　　　Rd. = Road
St. = Street (*or* Saint)

(3) 呼びかけの仕方

Dear (title) (name)：

主な例：　Dear Mr. Brown：　　　　　男性宛
　　　　　Dear Professor Smith：　　　大学の先生宛
　　　　　Dear Ms. Anderson,　　　　　女性宛（既婚・未婚を問わず）
　　　　　Dear Mr. and Mrs. Jones,　　 夫妻宛
　　　　　Dear Sir/Madam：　　　　　　宛て名の名前が不特定の時

(4) 結びの言葉

| Sincerely, | Very truly yours, | Yours truly, | Love, |
| Sincerely yours, | Cordially, | Yours sincerely, | Fondly, |

(5) 署　名

　結びの言葉の後に自分の名前をサインし、さらにその下に自分の名前をタイプで打つ。その際、自分の名前には通常タイトルはつけないが、外国人にとって自分の名前だけで、性別がわからないであろうと思われる場合は、下のように（　）の中にタイトルを示して相手が返事をする際、Mr. / Miss / Ms. の使用に関し、迷わないように配慮することもできる。

　　（Miss）Tomoko Saito

　　（Mr.）Tsutomu Yamaguchi

Rhetoric 3 — Resume（英文履歴書）の書き方

　英語で履歴書を書く場合、日本語の場合と違って所定の履歴書の用紙があるわけではないので、普通の A4 版の白い紙にモデル文のような様式に従って書く。

　書き方の注意事項としては次のとおりである。以下の ①〜④ はモデル文に示した ①〜④ に対応している。

① 英文の履歴書は resume という呼び方のほかに、personal experience, personal background, personal history, CV (Curriculum Vitae) というタイトルでも書かれることがある。

② 職歴と学歴は日本の履歴書とは逆の書き方をする。つまり英語では普通、職歴の方が学歴より先に書かれ、しかも書き方も現在から過去へさかのぼる書き方をする。

③ 学歴の欄にはその学校に通った期間、学位の種類、学校の名前、専攻を記す。学位の種類には次のようなものがある。

　　　　Associate of Arts degree（A. A.）：　　短期大学卒業
　　　　Bachelor of Arts degree（B. A.）：　　文科系大学卒業
　　　　Bachelor of Science degree（B. S.）：　理科系大学卒業

④ 求人側が望んだとき、応募者に関する照会状を書いてくれる人である。これも必要でないかぎり強いて書く必要はないものである。

RESUME①

Tomoko Saito
2-3, Midori-cho 1-chome
Koganei-shi, Tokyo
(090) 9685-22xx
saito@yahho.co.jp

Objective
To find a position in an international company where I can use English and business skills on a daily basis.

Work Experience②
April 2023-present: Part-time instructor at ABC English Academy, Tokyo, Japan
September 2022-March 2023: Interpreter registered with Tokyo Personpower Inc., Tokyo, Japan. Served as temporary secretary in a variety of offices and laboratories.
April 2022-August 2022: Part-time swimming instructor, Asia Swimming Club, Tokyo, Japan

Education③
April 2021-present: TSM University. Major: English Language. Expect to graduate in March 2025 with Bachelor of Arts degree.
March 2023: Certificate of Completion, English Instructor Program at ABC English Academy
April 2018-March 2021: Midori High School, Koganei-shi, Tokyo

Personal Achievements
December 2023: Best Teacher Award
November 2022: Society of Student Translators, President

References④
Mr. Tadashi Okamoto, Manager
ABC English Academy
(03) 3238-33xx
okamoto@yahho.ac.jp

On Your Own

Chapter 2 の Exercise 2 で書いた表をもとに、自分の英文の履歴書を作成してみよう。

Vocabulary ― カタカナ語

日本語には多くのカタカナ語があり、英語のように聞こえるものも多い。しかし、カタカナ語の中には、原語とは、発音も意味もずれているものが多いので注意したい。

Task 3

次のカタカナ語に相当する英語を書きなさい。

① アウトプット	② ウィルス	③ カンニング	④ テレビ
⑤ リモコン	⑥ ガソリンスタンド	⑦ アルバイト	

カタカナ語を大別すると次の7種類になる。

(1) 原語の英語にほぼ近いもの
　　専門用語は意味が限定されているので、原語とのずれが生じにくい。
　　　〔例〕　インプット：input　　モニター：monitor

(2) 原語の英語と意味は同じだが、発音がずれているもの
　　原語の英語の発音に注意したいものである。
　　　〔例〕　チップ：tip [tip] (cf. chip [tʃip]：切れ端)
　　　　　　エネルギー：energy [enərdʒi]

(3) 原語の英語と形は似ているが、意味がずれているもの
　　多くのカタカナ語がこれに属する。英作文の際には特に注意すべき部類である。
　　　〔例〕　サイン：　日本語　有名人のサイン
　　　　　　　　　　　英　語　autograph (cf. sign：署名する　signature：署名)

(4) 原語の英語の最初の部分を取ったもの
　　原語の頭の部分を取り、残りを省略したもので、「切り株語」と呼ばれる。
　　　〔例〕　インフレ：inflation　　スト：strike

(5) 原語である英語の複合語の一部をくっつけたもの
　　原語である複合語のそれぞれの語を切り取り、省略、合成により作ったもので、4音節のものが多い。
　　　〔例〕　プロレス：professional wrestling　　パソコン：personal computer

(6) 原語と思われている英語にはないもの
　　いわゆる和製英語と呼ばれるもので、英語としては意味の通じないものである。英作文をする際には落とし穴になるのがこの和製英語であるので注意したい。
　　　〔例〕　ゴールデン・タイム：prime time　　ナイター：night game

(7) 原語が英語ではないもの
　　英語以外の言語に由来するカタカナ語も多い。
　　　〔例〕　カルテ　medical record (cf. ドイツ語 Karte)
　　　　　　アンケート　questionnaire (cf. フランス語 enquête)

■コラム■

Story Grammar

まとまった筋を持つ物語を書く上で基本となる Story Grammar の要点を知っておこう。時間の流れに沿って書くという点では、Chapter 2 で学んだ手法をここでも活用することになる。

Task

次の各文を並べ換えて、「シンデレラ」の物語となるようにしなさい。

(a) When the clock struck midnight, Cinderella had to run away, with one of her glass slippers left behind.
(b) At last, he found Cinderella.
(c) She was sad and imagined what the ball would be like.
(d) The prince and Cinderella got married and lived happily ever after.
(e) She finally went to the ball and met the prince.
(f) Once upon a time there lived a girl named Cinderella, who was treated like a slave by her mean stepmother and stepsisters.
(g) The prince danced with Cinderella and fell in love with her.
(h) One day a prince invited all the ladies in the country to a ball at the palace, but Cinderella could not go as she had no dress to wear.
(i) The prince decided to find the girl whose foot fit the glass slipper.
(j) Then a fairy produced a beautiful dress and glass slippers for her with a magic wand and warned her to be back by midnight.
(k) He searched for the girl all over the country.

(　)→(　)→(　)→(　)→(　)→(　)→(　)→(　)→(　)→(　)→(　)

Story Grammar とは？

　私たちの祖先は、文字を発明する以前から、「もの」を話し言葉で「語る」ことによって「物語」を人から人へと伝えてきた。なぜこのようなことができたのだろうか。それは、物語が語り手にとっては語りやすく、聞き手にとっては理解し記憶しやすいような構造を持っていたからだと考えられている。この構造は **Story Grammar**（物語文法）と呼ばれ、普遍的なものとされている。この Story Grammar によって、「物語」は古今東西を問わず、人々の間で受け継がれていくことができたと思われる。

　さて Story Grammar とはこのように物語の基本的な構造だが、いくつかの構成要素から成り立っている。これらの構成要素のいずれかが欠けていると、物語は理解しにくくなってしまう。

(1) Story Grammar の構成要素

　Story Grammar は大きく分けて、物語の舞台となる設定を示す Setting（場面）と一連の Episode（挿話）から成る Event structure（出来事の構成）によって組立てられている。さらに Episode は、Beginning（発端）、Development（展開）、Ending（結末）から成っている。そして、Development は Reaction（登場人物の反応）と Goal path（解決への道）に、さらに、Goal path

はAttempt（試み）とOutcome（結果）から成る。

(2) Story Grammarによる物語の展開法

　Story Grammarは以下に示したように枝分かれした構造を持っていて、複雑な物語ほど、Event structureの部分に多くのEpisodeが埋め込まれている。

　なお、物語は下記の図の①→⑪という順序で展開する。通常、Settingに始まり、Episode 1のBeginning 1, Reaction 1, Attempt 1, Outcome 1, Ending 1と進み、次いでEpisode 2のBeginning 2, Reaction 2, Attempt 2, Outcome 2, Ending 2という順序で展開する。さらに複雑な物語になると、次にEpisode 3のBeginning 3, Reaction 3...という順序で展開することになる。

Story Grammarの構造

```
                          Story
                         /     \
                   Setting     Event structure
                     ①        /      |       \
                         Episode 1  Episode 2  Episode 3
                         /   |   \   /   |   \
                 Beginning 1 Development Ending 1  Beginning 2 Development Ending 2
                     ②      /    \      ⑥           ⑦         /    \       ⑪
                       Reaction 1 Goal path              Reaction 2 Goal path
                           ③     /    \                     ⑧     /    \
                            Attempt 1 Outcome 1              Attempt 2 Outcome 2
                               ④       ⑤                       ⑨       ⑩
```

(Carrell, 1984)

Exercise

　Taskで並べ換えた文を上記の枝分かれ図に当てはめた場合、①〜⑪に該当するものを記号で答えなさい。

　Story Grammarは物語の基本的構造であり、骨格に当たるものである。物語を書く場合には、Story Grammarに沿って書くことは必要条件であるが、それだけでは物語は無味乾燥なものとなってしまうので、骨格に肉付けをする必要がある。

　例えば、Taskで各文を並べ換えた「シンデレラ」の物語では、魔法使いのおばあさんがかぼちゃを馬車に変えたことや、王子様がどうやってシンデレラを見つけたかなどには触れてはいない。こうした内容は、Story Grammarの構成要素として必要なものではなかったからだ。しかし、こうした「+α」の部分は、Story Grammarに沿った骨格に対する肉付けとして、物語を生き生きとさせる大切な情報である。

List of Prefixes, Stems, and Suffixes

それぞれの単語例をいくつか挙げてみよう。

Prefix（接頭辞）	意　味	単語例
a-, an-	no, without	apathy,
ante-	before	anticipate,
bene-	well	beneficial,
bi-	two	bicycle,
by-	aside	byproduct,
circum-	around	circumstance,
contra-, anti-	against	contradict,
come-, con-, cor-, co-	together, with	combine,
de-	down from, away	detour,
dia-	through, across	diameter,
epi-	upon, over	episode,
hyper-	above, beyond	hypersensitive,
hypo-	under, beneath	hypothesis,
in-, im-	in, into, on	inspect,
in-, im-, il-, ir-	not	infamous,
micro-	small	microphone,
mis-	wrong	misfortune,
mono-	one	monopoly,
multi-	many	multiply,
peri-	around	periscope,
poly-	many	polyester,
pre-	before	predict,
post-	after	postpone,
re-, retro-	backward	retrospect,
semi-	half	semicircle,
sub-, suc-, suf-, sup-	under	subway,
super-	above, over	superficial,
syn-, sym-	with	sympathy,
trans-	across	transport,
tri-	three	triangle,
ultra-	beyond	ultramodern,
uni-	one	uniform,

Stems（語幹）	意　味	単語例
-anthro-, -anthrope-	man	anthropology,
-aster-, -astro-, -steller-	star	astronomy,
-audi-, -audit-	hear	audience,
-auto-	self	autograph,
-bio-	life	biology,
-capit-	head	capital,
-ced-	go, move	proceed,
-chron-	time	chronicle,

-corp-	body	corpse,
-cycle-	circle	tricycle,
-dic-, -dict-	say, speak	dictionary,
-duc-	lead	introduce,
-fact-, -fect-	make, do	manufacture,
-flect-	bend	deflect,
-gam-	marriage	bigamy,
-geo-	earth	geology,
-graph-, -gram-	write	telegram,
-hetero-	different	heterogeneous,
-homo-	same	homogeneous,
-hydr-, -hydro-	water	hydropower,
-log-, -ology-	speech, study	sociology,
-man-, -manu-	hand	manufacture,
-mega-	great	megaphone,
-metr-, -meter-	measure	kilometer,
-mit-, -miss-	send	transmit,
-morph-	form	amorphous,
-mort-	death	mortician,
-onym-, -nomen-	name	synonym,
-pathy-	feeling	sympathy,
-phil-	love	philosophy,
-phone-	sound	telephone,
-pod-, -ped-	foot	pedestrian,
-port-	carry	transport,
-psych-	mind	psychology,
-scrib-, -script-	write	scribble,
-seque-, -secut-	follow	sequence,
-soph-	wise	philosophy,
-spect-	look at	inspect,
-spir-	breath	inspire,
-tele-	far	telephone,
-therm-, -thermo-	heat	thermometer,
-vene-, -vent-	come	adventure,
-ver-	true	verify,

Suffix（接尾辞）	意　味	単語例
-al	（形容詞を作る）	loyal,
-active, -ive	（形容詞を作る）	attentive,
-ic	（形容詞を作る）	poetic,
-ous, -ious	（形容詞を作る）	nutritious,
-wise	（形容詞を作る）	clockwise,
-ian, -er, -or, -ist	（〜する人を表す）	comedian, painter, director, pianist
-tion,	（動詞から名詞を作る）	industrialization,

辞書を見てそのほかの prefix, stem, suffix 及びその用例を書き加えよう。

Revision Check List

優先順位	焦 点	チェック項目
1	内　容	● トピックに関連することを述べているか。 ● 読者にわかりやすいように、主題を明確に示しているか。 ● 主題を十分に発展させているか。 ● 論旨は終始一貫しているか。
2	構　成	● 導入部、本論、結論部という構成になっているか。 ● 導入部には主題文が明確に書かれているか。 ● 本論は主題文を十分に支持しているか。 ● 結論部は主題を繰り返し、文章全体を簡潔に要約しているか。 ● 導入部、本論、結論部はすべて主題と関連しているか。 ● 各パラグラフにはトピック・センテンスが明確に書かれているか。 ● 支持文はトピック・センテンスを十分に支持しているか。
3	文　章	● 各々の文は前後の文と論理的に、自然につながっているか。 ● 結束性は保たれているか（語彙の言い換え、代名詞、定冠詞、つなぎ言葉の使用は適切か）。 ● 統一性は保たれているか。
4	文	● 細切れの文になっていないか。 ● 受動態が不必要に多く使われていないか。
5	語　彙	● 適切な語彙が使われているか。 ● 形容詞の並べ方は適切か。 ● denotation と connotation は適切に使い分けられているか。 ● 接頭辞、接尾辞は正しく使われているか。 ● 類義語は適切に使い分けられているか。 ● 基本動詞は適切に使われているか。
6	文　法	● 時制は一致しているか。 ● 主語と動詞は呼応しているか。 ● 冠詞は正しく使われているか。 ● 前置詞は正しく使われているか。 ● 不定詞と動名詞の使い方に混乱はないか。
7	綴　字 句読点	● 綴字の誤りはないか。 ● 句読点の誤りはないか。

フリー・ライティング記録表

回	日付	トピック	語数	時間(分)	1分間の語数
1	/				
2	/				
3	/				
4	/				
5	/				
6	/				
7	/				
8	/				
9	/				
10	/				
11	/				
12	/				
13	/				
14	/				
15	/				
16	/				
17	/				
18	/				
19	/				
20	/				
21	/				
22	/				
23	/				
24	/				

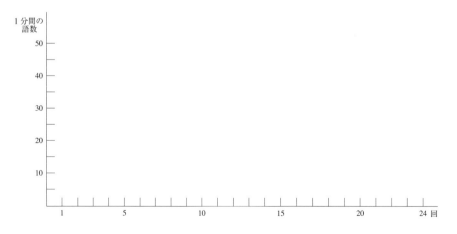

参 考 文 献

朝尾幸次郎『語彙・表現』（英語の演習 第3巻）大修館書店. 1985.
上村妙子・大井恭子『レポートライティング』日本英語教育協会. 1992.
國廣哲彌「意味と語彙」國廣哲彌（編）『日英語比較講座 第3巻』大修館書店. 1981.
小島義郎『日本語の意味　英語の意味』南雲堂. 1988.

Barnlund, D. C. (1988). *Communicative styles of Japanese and Americans: Images and realities*. Belmont, CA: Wadsworth Publishing Company.
Carrell, P. I. (1984). Evidence of a formal schema in second language comprehension. *Language Learning*, 34, 87–108.
Flexner, S. B. (Ed.) (1987). *The Random House dictionary of the English language*. New York: Random House.
Fry, E. (1992). *Doctor Fry's spelling book*. Lagna Beach, CA: Lagna Beach Educational Books.
Kaplan, R. B. (1966). Cultural thought patterns in inter-cultural education. *Language Learning*, 16, 1-20.
Oshima, A., & Hogue, A. (1991). *Introduction to academic writing*. Reading, MA: Addison-Wesley Publishing Company.
Rubin, J. (1975). What the 'good language learner' can teach us. *TESOL Quarterly*, 9, 41–51.
Summers, D. (Ed.) (1992). *Longman dictionary of English language and culture*. Harlow: Longman.
Summers, D. (Ed.) (2003). *Longman dictionary of contemporary English*. Harlow: Pearson Education limited.

《著者紹介》
大井恭子（おおい きょうこ）
　　東京大学文学部卒業。
　　ニューヨーク州立大学大学院言語学科博士課程修了。文学博士。
　　千葉大学名誉教授。

上村妙子（かみむら たえこ）
　　聖心女子大学文学部卒業。
　　ペンシルベニア州立インディアナ大学大学院言語学科博士課程修了。文学博士。
　　現在、専修大学文学部教授。

佐野キム・マリー（さの きむ まりー）
　　ミネソタ州立大学卒業（異文化間コミュニケーション専攻）。
　　テンプル大学大学院修士課程修了。文学修士。
　　現在、津田塾大学非常勤講師、東京女子大学非常勤講師。

KENKYUSHA
〈検印省略〉

Writing Power（Third Edition）
ライティング・パワー（三訂版）

2024 年 10 月 31 日　　　三訂版発行

著　者　大井恭子 / 上村妙子 / 佐野キム・マリー
発行者　吉田尚志
発行所　株式会社 研究社
　　　　〒102–8152 東京都千代田区富士見 2–11–3
　　　　電話　03–3288–7777（営業）
　　　　　　　03–3288–7711（編集）
　　　　振替　00150–9–26710
　　　　https://www.kenkyusha.co.jp/
印刷所　TOPPANクロレ株式会社

© Kyoko Oi, Taeko Kamimura, and Kim Marie Sano, 2024
装丁：株式会社明昌堂　本文イラスト：黒木ひとみ
音声吹込み・録音：Xanthe Smith, Peter Serafin
ISBN 978–4–327–42203–5　C1082　Printed in Japan

価格はカバーに表示してあります。
本書のコピー、スキャン、デジタル化等の無断複製は、著作権上の例外を除き、禁じられています。私的使用以外のいかなる電子的複製行為も一切認められていません。
乱丁本・落丁本はお取替えいたします。ただし、中古品についてはお取替えできません。